the Armenian
Genocide

ZORYAN INSTITUTE **SPECIAL REPORT NUMBER 3**

Hitler and the Armenian Genocide

KEVORK B. BARDAKJIAN

The Zoryan Institute

Cambridge, Massachusetts, 1985

The Zoryan Institute Special Report Number 3: *Hitler and the Armenian Genocide*

Published by The Zoryan Institute for Contemporary Armenian Research and Documentation, Inc. 85 Fayerweather Street, Cambridge, Mass. 02138

Printed in the United States of America
Transcript Printing Company, Peterborough, New Hampshire
Design by Tatul Sonentz-Papazian

ISBN 0-916431-18-5
Library of Congress Catalog Card Number 85-52406

Contents

In Memory of
Apkar Kapriel
&
Varteehad Sheklian
Omartian

I.

Introduction

"**Who,** after all, speaks today of the annihilation of the Armenians?" is a rhetorical question Hitler posed in a speech he gave to his military commanders on 22 August, 1939 in which he dealt mainly with his immediate plans for Poland. Within three days, on 25 August, 1939, a short account of the speech, smuggled out of the meeting, was transmitted to the British government by the British embassy in Berlin[1]. The same document was made public in the United States on 17 October, 1942, and *The New York Times* reported the story and excerpts from the document on the following day[2]. A little later in the same month, the entire text appeared in a book entitled *What About Germany?*[3] The US Department of Justice acquired a copy of the original in early 1944.[4] By the summer of 1945 the document was in the possession of the prosecution at Nuremberg, and by late November of the same year it made the headlines in the contemporary press and appeared in many books. Although the document served a useful purpose at Nuremberg, the sobering thoughts it had generated soon died away. A particular crime, the most horrendous in the history of mankind, had been dealt with; and that was that.

Few realized at the time, that the Holocaust was the latest in a chain of systematic butcheries that by now formed a clear pattern of increasing massive violence. Fewer still paused to place Hitler's utterance in its moral and historical context; to reflect upon the striking parallels between two premeditated crimes committed in the thick of two World Wars; to recall that an abortive "Nuremberg" had occurred about a quarter of a century earlier when an Ottoman Tribunal had sat in Istanbul to try Young Turk leaders for war crimes and crimes against the Armenians; and, to consider the chilling lessons Hitler had drawn from the Armenian Holocaust. But to the Armenians the cruel irony of Hitler's rhetorical question was hauntingly true: Hilter, not the world, had remembered their genocide for his own criminal purposes. The reference was all too disturbing to overlook; and the Armenians have accordingly underlined its moral and historical relevance, especially in view of the continuing denial of their genocide and of recurring instances of massive slaughter.

The prominence accorded to Hitler's words by the Armenians has recently given rise to renewed doubts questioning the authenticity of Hitler's statement. But it is not so much such challenges as the lack of documentation or, rather, the general lack of familiarity with pertinent documentation that motivated me to look into the matter. The literature on Hitler and Nazi Germany is overwhelmingly vast and complex, but my main concern in this booklet has been Hitler's views of the Armenians, particularly those related to the massacres, which remain almost totally unexplored. Although I have been able to accomplish my limited aim of tracing the origin and subsequent fate of the document containing Hitler's rhetorical question, and to locate some additional relevant material, there is still much to be done to elaborate on the issue and to answer numerous questions this preliminary investigation raises, especially with regard to the wider and inadequately explored context of Armenian-Turkish-German relations in the late-nineteenth and twentieth centuries.

KBB

II.

The Document

The story begins with the distinguished American journalist Louis Paul Lochner, who was the first to publish the document containing Hitler's rhetorical question. Born to the Reverend Frederick (a Lutheran) and Maria (von Haugwitz) Lochner in 1887 in Springfield, Illinois, he attended Milwaukee public schools, studied music at the Wisconsin Conservatory of Music, and in 1909 received his B.A. with Phi Beta Kappa honors from the University of Wisconsin.[5]

Although from 1909 to 1914 he was editor of the *Wisconsin Alumni Magazine* and the *Cosmopolitan Student,* his pacifistic activities soon overshadowed his literary efforts. He became lecturer for the extension division of his Alma Mater and for the American Peace Society, the Central-West department of which he later directed. In 1915 he accepted the position of secretary to Henry Ford and at the same time was secretary and press agent for the Ford Peace Ship. A year later he worked as secretary for the Neutral Conference for Continuous Mediation at Stockholm and the Hague.

Lochner returned to journalism in 1918 as editor of the International Labor News Service. Before joining the Berlin staff of the Associated Press in 1924 he worked as reporter on the old *Milwaukee Free Press. . .*

A master of the German language, Lochner built up an extensive network of contacts with high government officials. He obtained an exclusive interview with Marshal von Hindenburg in 1925 when the latter was candidate for President.[6]

From 1928 to 1941 Lochner was chief of the Berlin

Associated Press Bureau where he found himself in the midst of developments that led to the Second World War. During his tenure in Germany, he became President of the American Chamber of Commerce in Berlin (1935-1941) and President of the Association of Foreign Correspondents in Germany (1928-1931, 1934-1937).[7] His excellent reporting won him a Pulitzer Prize (1939) and his extensive travels enabled him to cover major events and diplomatic conferences in London, Geneva, Paris, and Rome. Lochner interviewed Hitler for the first time in early 1930.[8]

Before Hitler became the Chancellor of the German Reich, Lochner had another opportunity to interview him, and he also covered the famous purge in June 1934. He managed, however, to keep out of trouble with the Führer and his satellites, a fact which accounts for the many special permissions he was granted. He accompanied Hitler on his visit to Mussolini in 1938 and he was the first correspondent to be allowed to follow the German Army into Poland in September 1939, to go with the German Army through Holland, Belgium, and France the next year, and through Yugoslavia and Greece in 1941. In his last year he accompanied the Finnish Army into Russia.[9]

Throughout, Lochner maintained extensive, if discreet, ties with the German Resistance. In the Autumn of 1941, as he was shortly due to return to the United States, Lochner in a secret meeting with some members of the Resistance was entrusted with the task of providing President Roosevelt with information about the opposition to Hitler.[10] But, three days after the Japanese attack on Pearl Harbor, on 10 December, 1941, Lochner and his Associated Press colleagues and a number of other Americans were rounded up and interned for five months. Lochner arrived in New York on 1 June 1942 and was assigned to the Associated Press Bureau in Washington. He initiated contact with the White House but was unable to accomplish his mission due mainly to political considerations on the part of the United States government vis a vis the German Resistance of whose members and activities Washington was already well-informed.[11]

Five months after his return to the United States Lochner completed a book entitled *What About Germany?*,

which became a best seller and was published in England, Portugal and Sweden. Next Lochner went on a lecture tour of the

4

United States. Then between May, 1943, and October, 1944, he served as news commentator with NBC Pacific Coast and Rocky Mountain networks.

In 1944 Lochner returned to Europe as a war correspondent with instructions from A.P. to interpret the European scene in terms of his special knowledge of Germany. In 1945 and 1946 he was present at the Nuremberg trials.[12]

Lochner left the Associated Press in 1946 and joined the State Department in 1952. He then moved to the United Nations in 1958 and was a radio commentator from 1960 to 1963. Lochner died in 1975 in Wiesbaden, Germany where he had resided from 1971.[13]

Lochner wrote several books but the one immediately relevant to our topic is his *What About Germany?*, published in October, 1942. In this book Lochner made public a document which was given to him by an unnamed "informant". In fact the book opens with a description of the circumstances under which the document was delivered to him, followed by its content:

My informant seldom visited me, but when he came it was always on legitimate business which he was careful to announce in advance over our tapped telephone. Even today nobody in Germany suspects him. It was he who not only gave me the zero hour for the outbreak of World War II, but who later informed me of the exact day and minute for the attack on Crete. It was he too who, thirty days before Hitler started his offensive against Russia, revealed the day and hour — three A.M. on June 22, 1941 — when the Nazi wave would start to inundate the USSR.

A week before Hitler's assault on Poland, this man delivered to me a three-page typed manuscript. The document, written in German, is entitled, "Contents of Speech to the Supreme Commanders and Commanding Generals, Obersalzberg, August 22, 1939." It is one of the most sensational and at the same time, most revealing papers I own.

This is what Adolf Hitler told the army heads and commanding generals whom he summoned to his summer capital near Berchtesgaden:

"My decision to attack Poland was arrived at last spring. Originally, I feared that the political constellation would compel me to strike simultaneously at England, Russia, France, and Poland. Even this risk would have had to be taken.

"Ever since the autumn of 1938, and because I realized that Japan would not join us unconditionally and that Mussolini is threatened by that nit-wit of a king and the treasonable scoundrel of a crown prince, I decided to go with Stalin.

"In the last analysis, there are only three great statesmen in the

5

world, Stalin, I, and Mussolini. Mussolini is the weakest, for he has been unable to break the power of either the crown or the church. Stalin and I are the only ones who envisage the future and nothing but the future. Accordingly, I shall in a few weeks stretch out my hand to Stalin at the common German-Russian frontier and undertake the redistribution of the world with him.

"Our strength consists in our speed and in our brutality. Genghis Khan led millions of women and children to slaughter — with premeditation and a happy heart. History sees in him solely the founder of a state. It's a matter of indifference to me what a weak western European civilization will say about me.

"I have issued the command — and I'll have anybody who utters but one word of criticism executed by a firing squad — that our war aim does not consist in reaching certain lines, but in the physical destruction of the enemy. Accordingly, I have placed my death-head formations[1] in readiness — for the present only in the East — with orders to them to send to death mercilessly and without compassion, men, women, and children of Polish derivation and language. Only thus shall we gain the living space (Lebensraum) which we need. Who, after all, speaks today of the annihilation of the Armenians?

"Colonel-General von Brauchitsch has promised me to finish the war in Poland in a few weeks. Had he reported that I need two years or even only one year to do it, I should not have issued the order to march but should have allied myself temporarily with England instead of with Russia. For we are not in a position to carry on a long war.

"One thing is true: a new situation has now been created.[2] I got to know those wretched worms, Daladier and Chamberlain, in Munich. They will be too cowardly to attack. They won't go beyond a blockade. We, on the other hand, have our autarky (self-sufficiency) and the Russian raw materials.

"Poland will be depopulated and then settled by Germans. My pact with Poland[3] was, after all, intended only to gain time. And as for the rest, gentlemen, the same thing will occur as regards Russia that I have tested out (durchexerziert) in the case of Poland. After Stalin's death — he is a very sick man — we shall demolish the Soviet Union. The dawn of German domination of the world will then break.

"The little states cannot scare me. Since Kemal's death Turkey is being governed by cretins and semi-idiots. Carol of Rumania is a thoroughly corrupt slave of his sexual desires. The King of Belgium and the Nordic kings are soft jumping jacks, dependent upon the good digestion of their gorged and tired peoples.

"We shall have to count on Japan's reneging. I have given Japan a full year's time. The emperor is a counterpart of the last czar. Weak, cowardly, undecided. May he fall a victim to the revolution! My cooperation with Japan never was popular anyway.

"We shall continue to stir up unrest in the Far East and in Arabia. Let our mentality be that of lords of the creation (Herren) and let us see in these peoples, at best, lacquered semi-apes who crave to be flogged.

"The opportunity is favorable as never before. My only apprehension is that Chamberlain or some other such dirty cuss (Saukerl) may come at the last moment with proposals and appeasements. I'll throw such a fellow down the stairs, even if I have to kick him in the belly before all photographers.

"No, it's too late for that.[4] The attack upon and the annihilation of Poland begins early on Saturday. I'll let a couple of companies, dressed in Polish uniforms, make an assault in Upper Silesia or in the Protectorate. It's a matter of utter indifference to me whether or not the world believes me. The world believes in success alone.

"For you, gentlemen, glory and honor are in the offing, such as have not beckoned for centuries. Be tough! Be without compassion! Act more quickly and more brutally than the others! The citizens of western Europe must shudder in horror. That's the most humane method of conducting war, for that scares them off.

"The new method of conducting war corresponds to the new draft of the frontiers — one continuous rampart from Reval, Lublin, and Kosice to the mouth of the Danube. The rest will be awarded to the Russians. Ribbentrop has instructions to make every offer and to accept every demand.

"In the west I reserve to myself the fixing of the best strategic frontier. There one can operate with Protectorates, say of Holland, Belgium, French Lorraine.

"And now: at the enemy! In Warsaw we shall meet again and celebrate!" [See footnotes to this text at the end of Appendix I].

My informant confided to me that, after hearing this astounding speech, Goering, wild with enthusiasm, climbed on a table, rendered fervent thanks, and promised to carry out the bloodthirsty orders.

Fearing that the document might be discovered in my home, I took it to the American Embassy and asked for permission to deposit it there. I also suggested that its contents be communicated to the American government.

"Why, my dear fellow, that's dynamite," the American official exclaimed, startled, when I began to read it. "I don't dare keep it in this Embassy for even an hour. Please take it with you at once."

There was nothing left for me to do except to take it to my home until such time as I could arrange to get it out of the country. As there was always the possibility of an unannounced search, I scrawled across the manuscript with red pencil, *"Ein Stück gemeiner anti-Hitler Propaganda"* (A piece of low-down anti-Hilter propaganda). This is a subterfuge that I have employed in a number of cases, expressing pretended moral indignation over a document whose unexplained possession might prove embarrassing to me. Had a search been made and the document been found, I would, of course, have pleaded that the paper reached me anonymously by mail, and that my own attitude toward it was indicated by my red marginal note. I would also have pointed to other documents, displeasing to the Nazis, which I considered it my right and my journalistic duty to preserve in order to be aware of all sides of a question.

The speech may well have seemed to contain dynamite to the American embassy official who declined to have anything to do with it, for when I visited him that Friday, August 25, Hitler was still going through the motions of negotiating with the British government through Ambassador Nevile Henderson.[14]

For some reason, Lochner omitted to mention that he took a copy of the document to the British Embassy in Berlin as well; and that if the American "official" (i.e. Alexander C. Kirk, the chargé d'affaires)[15] declined to retain the document, Sir George Ogilvie-Forbes of the British Embassy forwarded an English version of the document to his government in London with the following covering letter:

> The Ambassador has seen the enclosed which was communicated to me by Lochner of the Associated Press of America. His informant is a Staff Officer who received it from one of the Generals present at the meeting who is alleged to have been horrified at what he heard and to have hoped for the curbing of a maniac. Lochner specially asked that his name should not be disclosed. It is interesting and tallies in several details with information from other sources.
>
> As the Ambassador is overwhelmed with visits from colleagues, he may not have time to send it by the bag he takes tomorrow and here it is for your private eye and such disposal as is fitting.[16]

Two days later, on 27 August, 1939, Ogilvie-Forbes informed London that Lochner had been to see him again, this time with information (which Ogilvie-Forbes transmitted "under all reserve") that an Air Force Officer "has confirmed the general sense of Hitler's speech under reference with an expression of regret that Göring should have behaved himself as described."[17] But the document's provenance remained a mystery, no doubt due to Lochner's unwillingness to divulge his source at the time. He smuggled the original to the United States and made it public a few days prior to its publication in his *What About Germany?*

Six years after its clandestine delivery to the West and three years after it had been made public, the document came into the possession of the prosecution at the Nuremberg Trials which Lochner attended.[18] The fate of the document and its somewhat complicated story unfold in the following passages lifted verbatim from the Nuremberg Records. It is important to note that the topic before the Tribunal in the quotations below was the premeditated nature of destructive war against Poland.

8

In the afternoon session on Monday, 26 November, 1945, Mr. Sidney S. Alderman (Associate Trial Counsel, United States) concluded his review of document L-79 (concerning the attack against Poland) and moved on to discuss a set of three "related" documents "constituting a single group", to substantiate the premeditated assault on Poland. The contents of all three documents represented a speech by Hitler to his military commanders delivered at Obersalzberg on 22 August, 1939. The first in the set was the "Lochner document" identified as L-3 or Exhibit USA-28 (hereafter L-3).[19] The other two texts represented Hitler's same speech in two parts and were identified as 798-PS or Exhibit USA-29 (entitled "Speech by the Führer to the Commanders in Chief on August 22, 1939"; hereafter 798-PS) and 1014-PS or Exhibit-USA-30 (entitled "Second Speech by the Führer on August 22, 1939"; hereafter 1014-PS).[20] The latter two make no reference to the Armenians; and, of the two, 1014-PS is textually far closer to L-3:

> MR. ALDERMAN: We think, as I have just said, that this document [L-79 or Exhibit USA-27] leaves nothing unproved in those allegations in the Indictment. It demonstrates that the Nazi conspirators were proceeding in accordance with a plan. It demonstrates the cold-blooded premeditation of the assault on Poland. It demonstrates that the questions concerning Danzig, which the Nazis had agitated with Poland as a political pretext, were not true questions, but were false issues, issues agitated to conceal their motive of aggressive expansion for food and "Lebensraum."
>
> In this presentation of condemning documents, concerning the initiation of war in September 1939, I must bring to the attention of the Tribunal a group of documents concerning an address by Hitler to his chief military commanders, at Obersalzberg on 22 August 1939, just one week prior to the launching of the attack on Poland.
>
> We have three of these documents, related and constituting a single group. The first one I do not intend to offer as evidence. The other two I shall offer.
>
> The reason for that is this: The first of the three documents came into our possession through the medium of an American newspaperman and purported to be original minutes of this meeting at Obersalzberg, transmitted to this American newspaperman by some other person; and we had no proof of the actual delivery to the intermediary by the person who took the notes. That document, therefore, merely served to alert our Prosecution to see if it could find something better. Fortunately, we did get the other two documents, which indicate that Hitler on that day made two speeches, perhaps one in the morning, one in the afternoon, as indicated by the original minutes, which we captured. By comparison

9

of those two documents with the first document, we concluded that the first document was a slightly garbled merger of the two speeches.

On 22 August 1939 Hitler had called together at Obersalzberg the three Supreme Commanders of the three branches of the Armed Forces, as well as the commanding generals bearing the title Commanders-in-Chief (Oberbefehlshaber).

I have indicated how, upon discovering this first document, the Prosecution set out to find better evidence of what happened on this day. In this the Prosecution succeeded. In the files of the OKW at Flensburg, the Oberkommando der Wehrmacht (Chief of the High Command of the Armed Forces), there were uncovered two speeches delivered by Hitler at Obersalzberg, on 22 August 1939. These are Documents Numbers 798-PS and 1014-PS, in our series of documents.

In order to keep serial numbers consecutive, if the Tribunal please, we have had the first document, which I do not intend to offer, marked for identification Exhibit USA-28. Accordingly, I offer the second document, 798-PS, in evidence as Exhibit USA-29, and the third document, 1014-PS, as Exhibit USA-30.

These are again, especially the first one, rather lengthy speeches, and I shall not necessarily read the entire speech.

Reading from 798-PS, which is Exhibit USA-29, the Führer speaks to the Commanders-in-Chief on 22 August 1939: "I have called you together . . . "

THE PRESIDENT: Is there anything to show where the speech took place?

MR. ALDERMAN: Obersalzberg.

THE PRESIDENT: How do you show that?

MR. ALDERMAN: You mean on the document?

THE PRESIDENT: Yes.

MR. ALDERMAN: I am afraid the indication "Obersalzberg" came from the first document which I have not offered in evidence. I have no doubt that the defendants will admit that Obersalzberg was the place of this speech.

The place is not very significant; it is the time.[21]

Göring's Defense Counsel objected to all three documents and made the following general remarks after Mr. Alderman had cited relevant passages from 798-PS and 1014-PS:

DR. OTTO STAHMER (Counsel for Defendant Göring): Mr. President, may I make a short statement on the two documents which have just been read. Both the documents which were read and also the third which was not read but to which reference was made, are not recognized by the Defense. I do not wish this objection to appear unjustified; may I therefore give this explanation:

Both the documents which were read contain a number of factual errors. They are not signed. Moreover, only one meeting took place, and that is the cause for the inaccuracy of these documents. No one present at that meeting was charged with taking down the events in the meeting stenographically, and since there are no signatures, it cannot be determined who wrote the documents and who is responsible for their reliability. The third document which was not read is, according to the photostatic copy in the Defense's document room, simply typewritten. There is no indication of place or time of execution.

THE PRESIDENT: Well, we have got nothing to do with the third document, because it has not been read.

DR. STAHMER: Mr. President, this document has nevertheless been published in the press and was apparently given to the press by the Prosecution. Consequently both the Defense and the defendants have a lively interest in giving a short explanation of the facts concerning these documents.

THE PRESIDENT: The Tribunal is trying this case in accordance with the evidence and not in accordance with what is in the press and the third document is not in evidence before us.

MR. ALDERMAN: May it please the Tribunal, I recognize that counsel wonder how these two documents which I have just read are in our hands. They come to us from an authentic source. They are German documents. They were found in the OKW files. If they aren't correct records of what occurred, it surprises us that with the great thoroughness with which the Germans kept accurate records, they would have had these records that didn't represent the truth in their OKW files.

THE PRESIDENT: Mr. Alderman, the Tribunal will of course hear what evidence the defendants choose to give with reference to the documents.

MR. ALDERMAN: It has occurred to me in that connection that if any of these defendants have in their possession what is a more correct transcription of the Führer's words on this occasion, the Court should consider that. On the other question referred to by counsel, I feel somewhat guilty. It is quite true that, by a mechanical slip, the press got the first document, which we never at all intended them to have. I feel somewhat responsible. It happened to be included in the document books that were handed up to the Court on Friday, [23 November, 1945] because we had only intended to refer to it and give it an identification mark and not to offer it. I had thought that no documents would be released to the press until they were actually offered in evidence. With as large an organization as we have, it is very difficult to police all those matters.[22]

Next to object was Dr. Walter Siemers (Defense Counsel for Erich Raeder) who on the one hundred and thirty-first day of the Trials on Thursday, 16 May, 1946 raised specific points to question the authenticity of the documents; requested that document 1014-PS be stricken from the record; and submitted, as Mr. Alderman had suggested, yet a fourth version of Hitler's speech written by Generaladmiral Hermann Böhm (document

Raeder-27).[23] Responding to Dr. Siemers's request to replace 1014-PS with Böhm's text, Sir David Maxwell-Fyfe (Deputy Chief Prosecutor for the United Kingdom) argued in favor of 1014-PS maintaining that both documents (i.e. 1014-PS and Böhm's version) conveyed the same vital thoughts. Then there followed the Tribunal's decision on the fate of Document 1014-PS:

DR. SIEMERS: Now I come to the third key document — namely, Hitler's speech before the commanders-in-chief on 22 August 1939, at Obersalzberg. There are two documents: Document 1014-PS and Document 798-PS. Document 1014-PS is Exhibit USA-30, in Raeder Document Book 10a, Page 269; and Document 798-PS is Exhibit USA-29, in Document Book 10a, Page 266. In regard to this Document 1014-PS, which I have here in the original in the form submitted by the Prosecution, I should like to make a formal request. This Number 1014-PS was read into the record in the afternoon session of 26 November 1945 (Volume II, Page 286). I object to the use of this document. I request that this document be stricken from the trial record for the following reason . . .

THE PRESIDENT: What document are you speaking about now, 1014-PS?

DR. SIEMERS: In Raeder Document Book 10a. Page 269, Exhibit USA-30.

THE PRESIDENT: Very well, what are your reasons?

DR. SIEMERS: The deficiencies which were already mentioned in the other transcripts are much greater here. This document is nothing but two pieces of paper headed "Second Speech by the Führer on 22 August 1939." The original has no heading, has no file number, no diary number, and no notice that it is secret: no signature, no date, no . . .

THE PRESIDENT: The Tribunal would like to look at the original. Yes, Dr. Siemers.

DR. SIEMERS: It has no date, no signature — in the original in the folder, it has no indication of where the document comes from. It is headed "Second Speech . . ." although it is certain that on this date Hitler made only one speech, and it is hardly 1½ pages long, although . . .

THE PRESIDENT: When you say it has no date, it is part of the document itself which says that it is the second speech of the Führer on the 22d of August 1939.

DR. SIEMERS: I said, Mr. President, it has a heading but no date.

THE PRESIDENT: But you said it has no date.

DR. SIEMERS: It has no date as to when these notes were put in writing. It has only the date of when the speech is supposed to have been made. On all documents which the Prosecution submitted, also in the case of minutes, you will find the date of the session and the date on which the minutes were set up; also the place where the minutes were set up, the name of the person who set it up, an indication that it is secret or something like that. Furthermore, it is certain that Hitler spoke for 2½ hours. I believe it is generally known that Hitler spoke very fast. It is quite out of the question that the minutes could be 1½ pages long if they are to give the meaning and the content, at least to some extent, of a speech which lasted 2½ hours. It is important — I may then refer to still another point. I will submit the original of Document 798-PS afterwards. I am no expert on handwriting or typewriters, but I notice that this document, which is also not signed, whose origin we do not know, is written on the same paper with the same typewriter.

THE PRESIDENT: You say we do not know where it has come from — it is a captured document covered by the affidavit which was made with reference to all other captured documents.

DR. SIEMERS: Well, but I would be grateful to the Prosecution if, in the case of such an important document, the Prosecution would be kind enough in order to determine the actual historical facts to indicate more exactly where it originates. Because it is not signed by Schmundt or Hossbach or anyone and has no number, it is only loose pages.

THE PRESIDENT: I do not know whether the Prosecution can do that, but it seems to me to be rather late in the day to ask for it.

DR. THOMAS J. DODD (Executive Trial Counsel for the United States): Mr. President, I do not know what the exact origin of this document is offhand, but I expect that we could probably get some information before the Tribunal if the Tribunal wishes us to do so. But as the President pointed out, it is a captured document and everything that counsel says about it seems to go to its weight rather than to its admissibility.

THE PRESIDENT: The Tribunal would like to know where the document was found, if that is possible.

MR. DODD: I will make an effort to find that out.

DR. SIEMERS: Mr. President, Mr. Dodd just pointed out that my objection comes rather late. I believe I recall correctly that repeated objections were raised . . .

THE PRESIDENT: I think it was I who pointed it out, not Mr. Dodd.

DR. SIEMERS: Excuse me. I believe I recall correctly that the Defense on several occasions raised objection during the Prosecution's case, and it was said that all statements could be made during the Defense's case at a later time — namely, when it is the defense counsel's turn to speak.

THE PRESIDENT: I only meant that it might not be possible at this stage to find out exactly where the document came from, whereas, if the question had been asked very much earlier in the Trial, it might have been very much easier. That is all I meant. Have you anything more to add upon why, in your opinion, this document should be stricken from the record?

DR. SIEMERS: I should like to point out, Mr. President, that I do not do it for formal reasons but rather for a very substantial reason. Most important words in this document have constantly been repeated by the Prosecution during these 5 or 6 months — namely, the words "Destruction of Poland, main objective . . . Aim: elimination of vital forces, not arrival at a certain line." These words were not spoken, and such a war aim the German commanders-in-chief would not have agreed to. For that reason it is important to ascertain whether this document is genuine.

In this connection, may I remind the Court that there is a third version of this speech as mentioned in this courtroom — namely, Document L-3, which is even worse than these and which was published by the press of the whole world. Wherever one spoke to anyone, this grotesque and brutal speech was brought up. For that reason it is in the interest of historical truth to ascertain whether Hitler spoke in this shocking way at this time. Actually, I admit he used many expressions which were severe, but he did not use such words, and this is of tremendous significance for the reputation of all the commanders who were present.

Let me point out the next words. They say expressly, "close your hearts against pity, brutal measures." Such words were not used. I will be in a position to prove this by another witness, Generaladmiral Böhm.

I therefore request the Court to decide on my request for striking this document from the record. I should like to point out that the document is mentioned in the record at many points. Should the honorable Court so wish, I would have to look for all the points. I have found only four or five in the German record. If necessary, I would give all the points in the English record. It was submitted on 26 November 1945, afternoon session (Volume II, Page 286).

THE PRESIDENT: I do not think you need bother to do that. You are now only upon the question of whether the document should be stricken from the record. If it were to be stricken from the record, we could find out where it is. Is that all you wish to say?

DR. SIEMERS: One question to Admiral Raeder. The words which I just read, "brutal measures, elimination of vital forces" — were these words used in Hitler's speech at that time?

RAEDER: In my opinion, no. I believe that the version submitted by Admiral Böhm, which he wrote down on the afternoon of the same day on the basis of his notes, is the version nearest to the truth.

DR. SIEMERS: Mr. President, in order to achieve clarity on this question, I submit as Exhibit Raeder-27, in Raeder Document Book 2, Page 144, an orderly reproduction of this speech.

RAEDER: May I also have Document Book 2?

DR. SIEMERS: This is the speech according to the manuscript of Generaladmiral Hermann Böhm. Generaladmiral Böhm was present at Hitler's speech on 22 August 1939 at Obersalzberg. He made the notes during the speech. He transcribed them in the present form on the same evening — that is, on 22 August 1939 — in the Vier Jahreszeiten Hotel in Munich. I have certified the correctness of the copy. The original is in the handwriting of Generaladmiral Böhm. Böhm has been called by me as a witness for various other questions. He will confirm that the speech was made in this form as I have submitted here. A comparison of the two documents shows that all terms, such as "brutal measures," are not contained in this speech. It shows further . . .

SIR DAVID MAXWELL-FYFE: Surely this part of Dr. Siemers' argument must go to weight. He has said that a comparison of the two documents shows such and such. I have just looked at the end of Admiral Böhm's affidavit and it contains, I should argue, every vital thought that is contained in Document 1014-PS. But whether it does or not, that is a matter of weight, surely. We cannot, in my respectful submission, go into intrinsic comparisons to decide the admissibility of the document. As I say, on that I should have a great deal to say by comparing the documents in detail. That is not before the Tribunal now.

THE PRESIDENT: Yes. The Tribunal was only wanting to hear whatever Dr. Siemers has got to say upon the subject.

DR. SIEMERS: A comparison of the document with Documents 798-PS, in the longer and better version, as the Prosecution submitted . . .

THE PRESIDENT: Dr. Siemers, as Sir David Maxwell-Fyfe has just pointed out, a mere comparison of the documents — of the two or three documents does not help us as to its admissibility. We know the facts about the document: It is a document in German, captured among German documents.

DR. SIEMERS: I understand. I made the statement only in order to show that I am not raising objections for formal reasons, but because the thing is actually of great importance. In proof of my . . .

THE PRESIDENT: Well, then, you will be able to urge that when you make your speech in criticism of the document as to its weight. You will be able to point out that it does not bear comparison with a fuller document taken down by Admiral Böhm or with the other document.

DR. SIEMERS: Absolutely right. To explain my formal request, I refer to my statement on the formal character of the document which I submitted.

THE PRESIDENT: Yes.

The application to strike out Document 1014-PS is denied.[24]

To recapitulate the story, L-3 (where Hitler's reference to the Armenians is found) was referred to by the prosecution but was not submitted in evidence for two reasons. The first reason was the lack of "proof of the actual delivery [of L-3] to the intermediary by the person who took the notes." The second reason was based on the prosecution's belief that Hitler had made not one, but two speeches on 22 August, 1939, and that, therefore, L-3 was a "slightly garbled merger of the two speeches" contained in Documents 798-PS and 1014-PS. On the other hand, the Defense held that Hitler had made but one long speech on that particular day, the most faithful reproduction of which was the account of Hermann Böhm. Eventually, only Documents 798-PS, 1014-PS and Raeder-27 (Böhm's version), none of which refers to the Armenians, were sumbitted in evidence. The central question that needs an answer is this: does the prosecution's decision to withdraw L-3 in any way diminish the value of this document?

To put the matter into its proper perspective, the provenace of L-3 must be established and the objectives of both the prosecution and defense must be clearly understood. At the same time, one must bear in mind that the search for additional evidence which led to the discovery of 798-PS and 1014-PS was prompted by L-3;[25] that the prosecution never questioned the overall authenticity of L-3; that the prosecution would certainly have used L-3 had it known its provenance or had it not stumbled upon 798-PS and 1014-PS; and that the prosecution, although never formally admitting it, withdrew L-3 simply because it had assembled enough evidence to build up its case regarding the assault on Poland.

To return to the objectives of both the prosecution and defense, through documents 798-PS and 1014-PS the prosecution tried to demonstrate: 1) that Hitler's attack on Poland was the result of a premeditated decision or a conspiracy to which the Nazi leadership was an accomplice; 2) that Hitler's ultimate goal was not just the military defeat of Poland, but its ruthless elimination as a vital force. The most damning evidence on this account was found in 1014-PS. But Hitler's same thoughts are also found in L-3 and another document. In order to substantiate my point that Hitler did indeed speak of his destructive intentions, all three documents must be examined. Juxtaposed below are the relevant and corresponding passages from L-3 and 1014-PS; and, the pertinent entries for 22 August, 1939 from the Notebook of Colonel General Halder, "which consists of shorthand notes made personally by Halder in connection with his daily tasks as chief of the General Staff of the Army" (this particular document surfaced after the Nuremberg Trials):

[FROM HALDER'S NOTEBOOK]

1) *Ruthless determination:* Anglo-French counter moves will come. We must stand fast. Build-up in West will go forward [W-*Aufmarsch wird gefahren*]. "Iron steadfastness of all in authority."

2) *Aim: Annihilation of Poland*—elimination of its vital forces. It is not a matter of gaining a specific line or a new frontier, but rather of the annihilation of an enemy, which must be constantly attempted by new ways.

3) *Solution:* Means immaterial. The victor is never called upon to vindicate his actions. We are not concerned with having justice on our side, but solely with victory.

4) *Execution:* Harsh and remorseless. Be steeled against all signs of compassion![26]

[FROM 1014-PS]

The destruction of Poland has priority. The aim is to eliminate active forces, not to reach a definite line. Even if war breaks out in the West, the destruction of Poland remains the priority. A quick decision in view of the season.

I shall give a propagandist reason for starting the war, no matter whether it is plausible or not. The victor will not be asked afterwards whether he told the truth or not. When starting and waging a war it is not right that matters, but victory.

Close your hearts to pity. Act brutally. Eighty million people must obtain what is their right. Their existence must be made secure.

The stronger man is right. The greatest harshness.[27]

[FROM L-3]

Our strength is in our quickness and our brutality. Ghengis Khan had millions of women and children killed by his own will and with a gay heart. History sees only in him a great state builder. What weak Western European civilization thinks about me does not matter. I have given the order and will have every one shot, who utters even one word of criticism that the aim of the war is not to attain certain lines, but consists in the physical destruction of the opponent. Thus for the time being I have sent to the East only my "Death's Head Units" with the order to kill without pity or mercy all men, women, and children of Polish race or language. Only in such a way will we win the vital space that we need. Who still talks nowadays of the extermination of the Armenians?[28]

17

All three passages unmistakably show, just as Hitler's subsequent record does, that the Führer had indeed planned a doomsday for Poland. Böhm himself, despite his pro-Hitler sympathy, offers further evidence in his carefully phrased account which, in Sir David Maxwell-Fyfe's words, includes "every vital thought that is contained in Document 1014-PS."[29] Even Dr. Siemers, Defense Counsel for Erich Raeder, admitted that Hitler in this meeting "used many expressions which were severe."[30] Dr. Siemers was very careful in his choice of words and it is easy to see through the phrase "many severe expressions" uttered by a Defense Counsel intent upon mitigating the crime and complicity of his client.

In contrast to the prosecution's attempt to prove the complicity of the Nazi criminals, the main thrust of Dr. Siemers's defense strategy was to dissociate them from the crime. His contention was that the Nazi defendants could not be regarded as accomplices to the conspiracy particularly in connection with the meeting at Obersalzberg on 22 August, 1939 where only Hitler had spoken and all those attending the gathering had simply listened to him. It is precisely with this purpose in mind that Dr. Siemers objected to 1014-PS holding that the words "Destruction of Poland, main objective . . . Aim: elimination of vital forces, not arrival at a certain line"[31] were not spoken; nor were the words "close your hearts against pity, brutal measures";[32] and that — and herein lies the clue to understanding Dr. Siemers's concern — "such a war aim the German commanders-in-chief would not have agreed to."[33]

Perhaps the best argument to refute Dr. Siemers's contention is that offered by Mr. Thomas J. Dodd (Executive Trial Counsel for the United States). Complying with the Tribunal's request to trace the origins of the documents, Mr. Dodd first made the following statement:

Mr. President, yesterday afternoon the Tribunal asked that we ascertain the origins, if possible, of Document 1014-PS. Some question was raised about it by Dr. Siemers. It is Exhibit USA-30.

I have had a search made, and I have some information that we are prepared to submit concerning this document. I should like to point out that 1014-PS and 798-PS and L-3 are documents all concerning this same speech made at Obersalzberg on 22 August 1939. They were offered in evidence by Mr. Alderman of the American staff on the 26th day of November 1945.

I should like to point out the L-3, to which Dr. Siemers made reference yesterday, was offered only for identification, as the record shows for the proceedings of that day on the 26th of November, and has received the mark Exhibit Number USA-28 for identification only. Mr. Alderman pointed out, as appears in the record, that he was not offering it in evidence, that it was a paper which came into our hands originally through the services of a newspaperman, and that later on the Documents 798-PS and 1014-PS were found among captured documents. They referred to the same speech in Obersalzberg. Mr. Alderman offered these two at that time.

Now Document 798-PS, Exhibit Number USA-29, and Document 1014-PS, Exhibit Number USA-30, were both found by the forces of the United States in this fashion:[34]

After describing how the documents had been found, Mr. Dodd added a few thoughts of his own:

Now, that is the history of these two documents about which Dr. Siemers raised some question yesterday — a considerable question I might say — and inferred there was something strange about their contents. I think the story which I have given in the form of a statement over the signature of Lieutenant Commander Hopper clearly establishes the source and where they have been ever since; and I think it is only fair to say that, since Dr. Siemers saw fit to point out that this language sounded extremely harsh and was attributed to Hitler, these documents were offered to show these people were actually talking about aggressive war. The reading of the three documents by the Tribunal will clearly show they are all in agreement in substance; of course, there are differences in phraseology, but the important thing and purpose for which they were offered was to show that these people were talking aggressive war. I might say I am not surprised to find my friend is sensitive about the remark, but I think the unanswered proof in the case thus far shows that not only were these things said but they were done.[35]

Dr. Siemers qualfied L-3 as a "grotesque and brutal speech."[36] Yet what the other documents convey and what Hitler in fact did in Poland and elsewhere are nothing short of grotesque and brutal; and it is only logical to conclude that a man capable of such cruel atrocities could have just as easily uttered such cruel words.

The next question awaiting an answer is the provenance of Document L-3. At Nuremberg, it was stated that it came into the possession of the prosecution:

through the medium of an American newspaperman and purported to be original minutes of this meeting at Obersalzberg, transmitted to this American newspaperman by some other person; and we had no proof of the actual delivery to the intermediary by the person who took the notes.[37]

19

A "person", then, who attended the meeting at Obersalzberg "took notes" and delivered his transcript or a copy of it to "some other person" or an "intermediary" who passed the document on to "an American newspaperman." Despite the omission of all names, at the time the prosecution was aware of the identities of both the American newspaperman and the intermediary. The newspaperman was Louis P. Lochner who, in a Testimony given in Berlin on 25 July, 1945, stated that the document was handed to him by Hermann Maass (the "intermediary") at the request of General Ludwig Beck, a former Chief of the German General Staff (1935-1938) and the highly respected leader of the anti-Hitler opposition.[38] Although a lesser figure, Hermann Maass (a former General Secretary of the "Reich Committee of German Youth Associations" and a co-founder of the "German Youth Radio")[39] was also an active anti-Nazi. Lochner further disclosed that Maass (and, incidentally, many others)[40] brought him authentic information from General Beck on previous occasions.[41] Responding to questions by his interrogator Colonel John H. Amen (Associate Trial Counsel, United States), Lochner thus described the circumstances under which the document had been entrusted to him:

Q Now, coming back to this particular manuscript of August 22 1939, when and under what circumstances was that first brought to your attention?
A Mr. Maasz came to me as he had often done before, into my office.
Q Where was your office located?
A That was down in Zimmer Strasse, SSE 68, in the newspaper row, where the various big concerns are. Opposite us was the German News Bureau and so on. He came to me and this day particularly was sure that the room was closed, and I had an inside office and nobody could see us, and then he produced this thing.
Q Was there anyone else in the room at the time?
A No, there was nobody with me. He produced it to me and first read it out to me and then when he came to a few words that I just don't know what they were, he took his scissors and cut those out and said, "Well, here is one name mentioned in here, and if ever this manuscript fell into the wrong hands, they would know where this comes from." It was evidently the person who took the stenogram of that meeting, and he cut that out, and after having read it out to me, he handed it to me, and I have been in possession of it ever since.[42]

Neither Lochner himself, nor, therefore, the prosecution knew the identity of the officer who had taken the notes and had passed them on to Beck who had arranged for their delivery to Lochner via Maass. For very good reasons, Maass had not revealed the original source to Lochner and had carefully excised the name from the document. Who could have been this person?

Although his identity has not been determined with absolute certainty, the original source of the document has been clearly established. Helmuth Groscurth, an Abwehr officer, has indicated in his "Diaries" that Admiral Wilhelm Canaris, head of Hitler's military intelligence, the Abwehr, attended the meeting and took notes.[43] Hans Bernd Gisevius (1904-1974), an active member of the German Resistance, has also attested that Canaris took his notes as Hitler spoke on 22 August, 1939:

> It was forbidden to make any copies of the speech before the briefing — for that was what it was. Canaris, who knew this fact, managed to sit in a corner where he could not be seen and take down the speech word for word. The very next day he read the most important passages to us. He was still utterly horrified. His voice trembled as he read. Canaris was acutely aware that he had been witness to a monstrous scene. We all agreed that this document of a time of delirium must be preserved for posterity. Another copy was, therefore, made from Canaris's entry in his journal, and Oster placed this copy in his collection of documents.[44]

Through a detailed historical and textual scrutiny of the numerous extant versions of Hitler's speech, Winfried Baumgart has established that documents 798-PS and 1014-PS originate from the Canaris notes (which no longer exist) and that L-3 can similarly be traced to the same source.[45] Winfried Baumgart's meticulous research and analysis, the testimony of contemporaries, and the almost total correspondence in contents of all three documents, leave no room for doubt that L-3 originated from the Canaris notes and that it was given to Beck most probably by Hans Oster, Chief of Staff to Admiral Canaris at the Abwehr and an intimate associate of both Canaris and Beck. Reconstructed, the chain of transmission must have involved, almost certainly, the following persons: Wilhelm Canaris — Hans Oster — Ludwig Beck — Hermann Maass — Louis P. Lochner.

The source of L-3 (and 798-PS and 1014-PS) thus traced, it is now a little simpler to deal with the prosecution's two main reasons for withdrawing L-3. Its first argument, that it found no proof of the actual delivery of L-3 to Hermann Maass, was somewhat inconsistent with its treatment of 798-PS and 1014-PS. Despite the fact that their provenance was unknown, the prosecution lent credibility to these two records simply because they had been found in the files of the OKW. Conversely, and despite the almost total correspondence in content of L-3 on the one hand and 798-PS and 1014-PS on the other, it withdrew the former on grounds that its origin was unknown. But its inconsistent approach and the availability of conclusive evidence apart, the prosecution's statement was a straightforward admission, made in good faith but with inadequate substantiation. For after questioning Lochner, the prosecution made no particular effort to find Maass, whose whereabouts or ultimate fate then remained unknown to interrogator and interrogated alike. Ironically, the prosecution would in no way have been able to verify the actual delivery of L-3 to Maass even if it had known the identity of the person who had taken the notes. By the time the Tribunal sat in Nuremberg, in fact even before the war ended, the four personalities connected with the three documents, Admiral Wilhelm Canaris (1887-9 April, 1945), Hans Oster (1888-9 April, 1945), Ludwig Beck (1880-1944), and Hermann Maass (1897-1944) had all been executed.

As for its second reason that L-3 was a "slightly garbled merger" of documents 798-PS and 1014-PS, the prosecution never substantiated its claim. Its assumption was based on the slight variations between the three documents and the failure of L-3 to distinguish two speeches by Hitler.[46] Insofar as it does not represent two separate harangues, L-3 may indeed be seen as a conflation the veracity of which we have no reason to question. Whether Hitler made one or two speeches on that particular day remains by and large a matter of interpretation, the only known fact being that his diatribe was interrupted by a short break. The issue, however, is an unimportant one. The imminent attack against Poland called for immediate action and the Resistance leaders could hardly have concerned themselves with such trivial details of format. "Utterly horrified" by the "monstrous scene"[47] he had witnessed Canaris, and his equally shaken collaborators hoped "for the curbing of a maniac"[48] before it was too late; and the condensed text prepared at the Abwehr faithfully relayed to the West Hitler's designs in Hitler's own words.

There is no reason, let alone evidence, to suggest that L-3 was "slightly garbled" (whatever the prosecution meant by this word). But even if we assumed, for the sake of the argument, that some of Hitler's views (e.g. those about statesmen) could conceivably have been painted in thicker colors, the historical facts and analogies he referred to could decidedly not have been "colored" simply because they do not lend themselves to such embellishment. What additional information L-3 has retained must have come from Canaris's fresh memory, if not from his original notes. There is no "official" record of Hitler's speech; and, although all the documents are almost identical in content, they naturally manifest slight variations in style and retain or omit certain points without contradicting one another. Furthermore, they are all summaries, none of which reports everything Hitler said. Thus, it is known for certain that Hitler on this occasion spoke at great length (at least "2½ hours" according to Dr. Siemers),[49] yet any of the texts can be read within a matter of minutes. Needless to say, had there been other versions, such texts would no doubt have preserved numerous expressions not found in any of the extant records. But Halder's Notebook consists of laconic entries. Böhm's statement, of which the original notes no longer exist, is the brief and carefully formulated account of a man who admired Hitler. By contrast, similar summaries though they are, documents 798-PS, 1014-PS and L-3, all of which come from the same source, faithfully represent Hitler's jargon. Whereas the former two were deposited in the OKW files and were, therefore, more "sober" in tone, L-3 was intended for the West and reproduced some of the vivid expressions and historical parallels Hitler was so fond of making. Given Hitler's true motives for the assault on Poland and the opposition he had earlier encountered from the military on the Czechoslovakian question, it was only logical for the Führer to cite historical evidence to justify his aims and to persuade his hesitant generals. After all, his designs for Poland called for cold-blooded measures similar to those applied by the Young Turks against the Armenians. One need only point to some specific parallels between the two cases: extermination of the intelligentsia, and mass deportations and massacres with the ultimate goal of Turkifying/Germanizing entire regions. Moreover, Hitler could hardly have found a better instance of mass murder to hammer home the idea that the world would turn a blind eye to the destruction of Poland in the same way as it had to the Armenian massacres.

To conclude, although its author is unknown, L-3 and its unsigned counterparts 798-PS and 1014-PS originate from the notes Wilhelm Canaris took personally as Hitler spoke on 22 August, 1939. The prosecution's decision at Nuremberg to withhold L-3 was therefore based on inadequate information, and remains irrelevant to the authenticity of L-3. Although not an "official" record, L-3 is a genuine document and is as sound as the other evidence submitted at Nuremberg.

III.

The Antecedent

Hitler's rhetorical question was not an isolated or a fortuitous remark. It had at least one identical precedent. The two references Hitler made to the Armenian genocide must be seen in the wider context of his thought, dominated from the outset by anti-semitism, a belief in Aryan supremacy and a drive for the acquisition of *Lebensraum*. His own destructive bent aside, Hitler's plans for the expansion and regrouping of the Germanic peoples would of necessity have compelled him to turn to history for instances of forcible resettlement, deportations, and massacres. Consider as he did past measures of atrocity, it should come as no surprise that the extermination of the Armenians also loomed large in Hitler's mind; it was, after all, the largest and freshest in human memory and, perhaps more important still, it had been perpetrated with impunity. The document to be discussed below is an independent piece of evidence and carries its own weight. Not only does it cast a light on the earlier stages of Hitler's ultimate objectives, it also establishes the historical background to his reference to the Armenians and proves, beyond doubt, that his rhetorical question came as an inescapable conclusion to his familiarity with the Armenian genocide as a case in point.

In 1931, Hitler granted two confidential interviews to Richard Breiting, editor of the *Leipziger Neueste Nachrichten,* "a great German daily newspaper" which "represented the policy of the conservative Right, the German National Peoples Party and the right wing of the German Peoples Party."[50]

When Hitler decided that the time had come to assault the bourgeois press fortress, he already had a strong organisation and a number of newspapers which were feared rather than respected. Many people, intimidated by the Gau papers and their attacks, were persuaded to fill the Nazi Party coffers. Hitler had perceived that the major newspapers acted as efficient links between industry, finance, the Wehrmacht, the Herrenklub, the intellectuals, the senior State authorities and the bourgeois section of the electorate. At this stage of his struggle it was important to him to harness these circles to his purposes. Tactically he preferred to make temporary allies of his opponents. He therefore set out to obtain the goodwill of influential key figures among the conservatives by talking of the 'legality' of his road to power. Demagogic speeches were of no use here; he could only convince by explaining his tactics, the precision of his calculations and insisting on the inevitability of historical developments. He wished to turn accomplices into conspirators. This can be the only explanation for the fact that, under ban of secrecy, he revealed matters which might have been dangerous to him had they become public knowledge.[51]

It is with these objectives in mind that Hitler held two confidential sessions with Breiting, "the all-powerful ruler of Leipzig's bourgeois parties."[52] The first one occurred on 4 May, 1931 and the second in early June of the same year. Breiting was allowed to take short-hand notes after being sworn to secrecy.[53] Some three years later (on 18 February, 1934, to be exact), the Gestapo requested the return of Breiting's notes,

on the grounds that they dealt with Hitler's thinking and that, should they become known, statements by the Führer before the seizure of power might be misinterpreted abroad. Breiting stated categorically that he had no papers and had destroyed his notes.[54]

When Hitler came to power, Breiting tried to join the Nazi party "to protect himself and his friends from persecution."[55] But he was branded a "Jewish lackey" and his application was turned down.[56] Moreover, he was threatened with legal action for "corruption and peculation",[57] and was soon liquidated:

On 19 April 1937 Breiting was summoned to the Reich Ministry of Propaganda in Berlin, where two Gestapo agents took him to a restaurant for a talk. Although he was only 54 and had hitherto been in good health, he returned to Leipzig racked with convulsions and a nervous fever. According to his family he was convinced that he had been poisoned. A week later he was dead. Though the family requested an autopsy, the doctor in charge refused. His body was cremated without his family's knowledge.[58]

It the first interview, Hitler spoke about his plans for the future, for the seizure of power, and for the total transformation of public life in Germany. In short, he dealt with internal affairs.

In the second interview he discussed his external policy and his plans for the transformation of Europe. Essentially, he said, he would fight Communism and Jewry; would abolish the humiliating terms of the Versailles *Diktat;* and would create a new order in Europe. Germany would be rearmed and would pursue a world policy. The Germanic peoples would be regrouped and Germany would acquire *Lebensraum* in Europe as well as in the East. His plans for the new order he proposed for Europe called for the abolition as states of Austria, Switzerland, Belgium, Yugoslavia, and Czechoslovakia. He expected no opposition from Britain (which was a "natural ally"), France, and the Catholic Church, because he did "not intend to tilt at windmills like Cervantes' hero" nor "to behave like a bull in a china shop."[59] The Americans were "a long way off geographically and we can do much to assist them to remain in isolation."[60] But, Hitler continued,

> we cannot stand idly by and watch what is taking place in Russia, for that is happening on our own continent. The most dangerous force in the world is Russian imperialism, Slav imperialism in combination with the dictatorship of the proletariat. If that symbiosis should come to pass ... Think of the reservoir of manpower and raw material resources at Stalin's disposal![61]

Having outlined his minutely considered plans for the future of Europe, Hitler then elaborated on a point which is of cardinal importance to our topic. He spoke of Germany's need for living space and for raw materials and their "equitable" distribution. He expressed his determination to colonize the East "ruthlessly" and to have "millions of men" resettled. Past instances of resettlement, "migrations", "deportations", and "massacres", which Hitler cited, justified his deadly plans and inspired his macabre imagination. This is how he built up his argument, jumping from one idea to another, but concluding with his "great resettlement policy":

> Our publicity men should already be thumping the drum today. The menace to western civilisation was never so great. Even before we assume power we must make clear to the British, French and Americans and the Vatican too that sooner or later we shall be forced to conduct a crusade against bolshevism. England and France

should be grateful to us for having recognised the danger in time. What does it matter to them who rules in Russia tomorrow? We must already be thinking of the resettlement of millions of men from Germany and Europe. Migrations of peoples have always taken place. In the single year 1641 *(sic)* 50,000 Irishmen left for North America and two-thirds of the country remained uninhabited. What a lot of nordic blood has flowed to the United States. We must colonise the East ruthlessly. Moreover we must not forget the world distribution of raw materials. Look at what is happening in Latin America. I have to thank my friend Ernst Röhm, the Chief of Staff, for the fact that I am well informed about conditions in Bolivia; he was a military instructor there. The country is rich in lead, copper, zinc, wolfram and gold. Nevertheless it lacks iron and coal. England and America may dominate world trade today but our trading capacity will change once we rule the eastern area. We think of a white South Africa, a white Australia and New Zealand, but we cannot countenance anything but a white Ukraine and a white Caucasus. How should the Portuguese and Spaniards continue to colonise Africa and South America when their resources are so small because they have no home industries. We would be glad to help them. Our prestige in South America is great. Many of Röhm's letters told me so. Unfortunately the sources of raw materials there are in the hands of Anglo-Saxon plutocracy and it is acting unreasonably. Think of the turn-over of Royal Dutch Shell, Anglo-Iranian Oil or Katanga Union and then compare our geographical possibilities in the East. The Middle East is not far off either. One of the Hohenzollerns launched the idea of the Berlin-Baghdad railway and people like von Papen fought for it in Palestine. Are we really to remain a nation of have-nots for ever? Why should not the sources of raw materials be equitably distributed? We have the capacity to rouse and lead the masses against this situation. In the long term ought Germany to be ground down economically? Everywhere there is discontent. Everywhere people are awaiting a new world order. We intend to introduce a great resettlement policy; we do not wish to go on treading on each other's toes in Germany. In 1923 little Greece could resettle a million men. Think of the biblical deportations and the massacres of the Middle Ages (Rosenberg refers to them) and **remember the extermination of the Armenians.** One eventually reaches the conclusion that masses of men are mere biological plasticine. We will not allow ourselves to be turned into niggers as the French tried to do after 1918. The nordic blood available in England, northern France and North America will eventually go with us to reorganise the world. The discontent in their own home countries and in their colonies will leave them no choice.[62]

Hitler's statement to Breiting is in itself a formidable document, revealing and incriminating. Its significance, needless to say, goes well beyond its intrinsic value in that it provides us with an insight into the roots of his rhetorical question found in L-3. But there is also a sequel to the story. Hitler in 1943 confirmed in deed what he had said in words.

IV.

The Sequel

It is well known that the Jews headed Hitler's hate-list, followed by the Slavs, Gypsies, and other so-called inferior races. But a cursory search into some Hitler-related documents has revealed that the Armenians too belonged to this group. In fact, in a few documents the Armenians hold the dubious distinction of running not too distant a second to the Jews. The OKH (Oberkommando des Heeres or The High Command of the Army), for instance, shared Hitler's utter contempt and held that the "Armenians were even worse than Jews."[63] Alfred Rosenberg, the ideologist of Nazism, classed the Armenians with "the people of the wastes, Jews, Armenians . . ."[64] Echoing Rosenberg's "racial" and racist views, Hitler on one occasion made the following statement:

> Considering that only a pure consciousness of racism can ensure the survival of our race, we were constrained to introduce racial legislation in such a clear way that such legislation could eliminate all alien racial infection, and this infection is not caused only by Jews. In enlightening the German people with regard to this racial legislation, we should conceive of it as having the task of protecting the German blood from contamination, not only of the Jewish but also of the Armenian blood.[65]

Obviously given to Rosenberg's "Aryan" fallacy which, among other things, maintained that the Persians had once been a truly "Aryan" race who were later "bastardized" and fell into decline, a muddle-headed Hitler made the following jumbled observation:

The Jews did not even possess organizational value. In spite of the fears which he, the Führer, had heard repeatedly in Germany, everything continued to go its normal way without the Jews. Where the Jews were left to themselves, as for instance in Poland, the most terrible misery and decay prevailed. They are just pure parasites. In Poland, this state of affairs had been fundamentally cleared up. If the Jews there did not want to work, they were shot. If they could not work, they had to perish. They had to be treated like tuberculosis bacilli, with which a healthy body may become infected. This was not cruel — if one remembers that even innocent creatures of nature, such as hares and deer, have to be killed so that no harm is caused by them. Why should the beasts who wanted to bring us Bolshevism be more preserved? Nations which do not rid themselves of Jews perish. One of the most famous examples is the downfall of that people who were once so proud, the Persians, who now lead a pitiful existence as Armenians.[66]

Hitler's chilling reflections and analogies deserve no further discussion. His contempt for the Armenians, and all other so-called inferior peoples, was as much the result of hateful racism as of his crass ignorance. If, however, he knew next to nothing about the history of the Armenians as a people, he was knowledgeable about their carnage in the years 1915-1916. A contemporary of the Armenian massacres, Hitler had fought in the First World War and could hardly have remained oblivious to the slaughter. The wholesale butchery of the Armenians was common knowledge in Germany, particularly in the years immediately following the war, through such sources as eye-witness accounts by German missionaries, teachers, businessmen, doctors, nurses, engineers, military personnel and diplomats in the Ottoman empire; books and articles; and the trial and acquittal in Berlin of Soghomon Tehlirian (1896-1960) who had gunned down Talaat, the former Young Turk interior minister and grand vizier of the Ottoman empire, as one of the principal organizers of the Armenian deportations and massacres. Hitler was in Berlin when this trial took place in the early part of June, 1921.[67] But apart from such public knowledge, Hitler must have heard the details of the story from an even better source of information, Max Erwin von Scheubner-Richter who

like so many other German officials in wartime Turkey, later became a prominent figure in German politics. In the early years of the Nazi movement he was one of Hitler's closest advisers and was killed at his side in the Munich Putsch of November 9, 1923.[68]

31

How close had Hitler and Scheubner-Richter been? In Robert
Cecil's words,

> Of the sixteen Nazi dead [during the Munich Putsch] he earned
> the finest epitaph from his surviving Fuehrer: "All are replaceable,
> but for one: Scheubner-Richter."[68]

Scheubner-Richter was the German vice-consul in Erzerum
from about the middle of February to early August, 1915 and fil-
ed numerous dispatches about the "terrible" misery and
"senseless" expulsion[70] and "anti-Armenian outrages"[71] in the
Armenian provinces. Hitler must have heard something from
his closest adviser and collaborator who had personally
witnessed the systematic deportation and slaughter of the
Armenians. He must have also heard something about the Pan-
Turanian movement which toward the end of the First World
War opened a wide gulf between the two allies: Germany and
the Ottoman Empire.[72]

The Committee of Union and Progress which ruled the Ottoman Empire from 1908 to 1918,

> made Pan-Turanism, that is the unity of all Turks in one country
> named Turan, a cardinal point of its foreign policy in the period
> 1908-1918.[73]

This statement would be closer to the truth if we added that
Pan-Turanism was made a cardinal point of internal Young
Turk policy as well; and that it in large measure accounted for
the Young Turk government's decision to deport and massacre
the Armenians. The Young Turk program called for the creation of a Turkish (Turanian) empire extending from the Balkans
to Central Asia and the Armenians were in the way. For "the
way to Turan"[74] passed through Armenia in the east and the
Young Turks dragged the empire into the First World War with
"Turan" in mind:

> The Ottoman Empire's entry into the first World War on the side
> of Germany was motivated, as is well known, in great part by the
> Young Turks' dream of acquiring territories inhabited by Turkic
> groups in Russia and the Balkans.[75]

In pursuit of the Pan-Turanian fantasy, Enver, the Ottoman
minister of war, personally commanded the Turkish offensive
eastward only to suffer perhaps the worst defeat in his entire
military career with tragic consequences to the Turkish soldier.
But the Bolshevik revolution completely changed the fortunes
of the war and the Ottomans' renewed attempt in the final

stages of the First World War to penetrate into the Caucasus and beyond was opposed by their allies, the Germans, on two accounts. In the first place, the Germans had their own designs for the Caucasus and Central Asia which conflicted with the Pan-Turanist dream. In the second place, the Germans feared, at least so they professed, that the Turks might resume the massacre of the remnants of the Armenians. The conflict became an irrelevant issue with the defeat of both powers in the First World War. After the war, "The Republican regime [in Turkey], established formally in 1923, repeatedly repudiated Pan-Turanism or Pan-Turkism."[76] But,

> Between 1941 and 1944, Turkey witnessed a resurgence of Pan-Turanism, now called Pan-Turkism, under German influence, which was brought under control through suppression of existing organizations and arrest of leaders.[77]

Of course there was more to this revival than just German influence. There was a lively, if discreet, official Turkish interest in territorial expansion. The "suppression of existing organizations and arrest of leaders" were temporary measures, dictated by political considerations, and the sentences were all eventually cancelled. But the movement is a complex issue and any discussion of it would necessarily require a review of a host of factors which are beyond the scope of this booklet. The Turkish attitude has been best summed up by C.W. Hostler:

> One may conclude that highly placed persons in the Turkish state had plans ready to exploit all the possibilities the German-Soviet war and a collapse of the USSR could furnish for the realization of Pan-Turkish ideals.[78]

More relevant to our topic is the German connection. While promoting Pan-Turanism,

> German intentions from the outset were unclear and were in reality aimed at a double game. The Germans hoped to exploit Turkish and Turko-Tatar assistance in the liquidation of the Soviet empire and to leave in German hands the future of the huge Soviet Russian colonies.[79]

Moreover, there were within the Nazi apparatus two conflicting attitudes toward Pan-Turanism. Unlike the Foreign Ministry and the German High Command, Alfred Rosenberg, then the *Reichsminister* for the German occupied territories in the East, was opposed to the movement. On at least two occasions, he privately expressed fears of its revival. In both instances, the discussion between him and the Führer revolved around the auxiliary forces which Germany proposed to recruit from various ethnic groups.

I further asked the Fuehrer if he had scrutinized the memoir on the establishment of Turkish legions. What I surmise, since the High Command of the Armed Forces (OKW) issued an order, is that beside the Turkish-Aserbeidschander Legion, other Caucasian legions will be set up also. The Fuehrer affirmed the question, and I once more referred to the danger of a panturanian movement.[80]

The second occasion arose about five months later, on 8 May, 1942:

Then the discussion turned to Caucasia and *the policy of the AA* [Foreign Ministry] towards the Eastern territories. I reported to the Fuehrer that, for some time, we had picked out the best of the prisoners by commissions of the Ministry East. The OKW had now established the Turkestan Legion through direct collaboration with us. According to my information received from the manager of chief section "Policy", the camp is in perfect condition, the Commander has learned the Turkestan language, and the Turkestans have accepted German military terms and have an anti-Bolshevist attitude. The legions of the Caucasians would be modeled on similar lines. If one had not in the beginning on the part of the SD, called all those peoples "Asiatics", had them shot or left to their fate, there would be more troops at the disposal of the German Reich today. A new flag was created for the Turkestan legion, the half moon was done away with and in its place put bow and arrow. I showed the Fuehrer the individual symbols for the designs for flags for the Georgians, Armenians, Aserbeidschanians, Cubancossacks, and Kalmucks. The Fuehrer had no objections against these designs, however, he asked my opinion about the Armenians. I stated that Armenia was the best bolt between Turkey and Aserbeidschan, and thus could stop a Pan-turanian movement towards the East. Generally speaking the Armenian people themselves are stationary, a people of farmers who had considerable industrial skill.[81]

Rosenberg's view of the Armenians had not changed and his somewhat favorable words were uttered to promote his own scheme for the region. But the war situation had changed drastically. As the Germans suffered setbacks both the pressure they had been applying to the Turks to join the Axis powers and their Pan-Turanist propaganda intensified,[82] despite Rosenberg's reservations. Hitler had earlier met with Pan-Turkists in Berlin and the Germans soon made "most tempting offers"[83] to the Turks, "holding out the Pan-Turanian dream",[84] "with a view to territorial aggrandizement."[85] By early 1943, as they most eagerly sought to win the Turks over, someone came up with an imaginative inducement of high political and ideological significance. On or just before 25 February, 1943, Talaat's body arrived at the Sirkeci station in Istanbul in a special wagon attached to the express train from Berlin.[85] Hitler, or whoever conceived the idea, could have thought of no better gesture to foster Pan-Turanism and to tempt the cautious Turks with the prospect of territorial expansion. Implied by this act was also a tacit approval of the violent ways in which the Young Turks had eliminated the Armenians during the First World War in pursuit of their Pan-Turanian fantasy and empire. For, then as now, the way to Turan passed through what remained of Armenia, now a Soviet republic. And Talaat, who had been "left with the responsibility for the implementation"[87] of the Ottoman government's decision to deport and massacre the Armenians, was, along with his Young Turk collaborators, the very epitome of this policy. Indeed, Talaat was, as Count Wolff-Metternich, the then German ambassador to Istanbul (November, 1915-September, 1916), put it, "the soul of the Armenian persecutions."[88]

Curiously enough, no one seems to know on whose initiative Talaat's body was returned **at this particular juncture.** Franz von Papen, the German ambassador in Turkey from 1939 to 1944 makes no mention of the event in his memoirs.[89] Yet, it would be illogical to suggest that the ambassador was unaware of the story and its details, particularly in view of the fact that his excellency was fully involved in German schemes to foster Pan-Turanism. As C.W. Hostler notes, "There were . . . meetings involving Pan-Turkists in Berlin in the latter part of 1941 attended by Hitler, von Papen and Nuri Pasha [brother of Enver]."[90] The numerous secret dispatches compiled by this ambassador also reveal his active role.[91]

A fairly extensive, but not exhaustive, research into German documents yielded no results either. Perhaps more curiously, Talaat's own biographer has professed to be unaware of the origins of the story. He states that in February, 1943, "Hitler's government" decided to return Talaat's body but that it is unknown on whose initiative. The suggestion, he maintains rightly, could have come from either government: the German, in view of the disastrous reverses its armies were suffering at the time; or the Turkish government which might have thought that the time had come for the return of Talaat's body.[92] Talaat's "repatriation" would not have been possible under Atatürk, whose regime had been hostile to the Young Turks. But he was gone, and a different man, Inönü who was far more favorably disposed toward the Young Turks than Atatürk had been, was now at the helm. Nevertheless, it would be more sensible to speculate that it was Hitler or his "government" that conceived of the idea fully realizing the symbolic significance of the gesture.

It now seems inevitable to conclude this inquiry with a "platitude" recited all too frequently in recent times. But one has no choice, unless, that is, one is prepared to commit to oblivion all past instances of deliberate murder by substituting "the Armenians" in Hitler's rhetorical question with "the Jews", "the Cambodians" and who knows with whom else yet. It is with such concerns uppermost in his mind that Justice Robert H. Jackson, Chief-of-Counsel for the United States, began his closing arguments at the Nuremberg Trials. His words, which encompassed the Armenians as well, may sound "old"; but they are certainly, though most regrettably, as valid as ever:

Mr. President and Members of the Tribunal: An advocate can be confronted with few more formidable tasks than to select his closing arguments where there is great disparity between his appropriate time and his available material. In 8 months — a short time as state trials go — we have introduced evidence which embraces as vast and varied a panorama of events as has ever been compressed within the framework of a litigation. It is impossible in summation to do more than outline with bold strokes the vitals of this Trial's mad and melancholy record, which will live as the historical text of the twentieth century's shame and depravity.

It is common to think of our own time as standing at the apex of civilization, from which the deficiencies of preceding ages may patronizingly be viewed in the light of what is assumed to be "progress." The reality is that in the long perspective of history the present century will not hold an admirable position, unless its second half is to redeem its first. These two-score years in the twentieth century will be recorded in the book of years as one of the most bloody in all annals. Two World Wars have left a legacy of dead which number more than all the armies engaged in any way that made ancient or medieval history. *No half-century ever witnessed slaughter on such a scale, such cruelties and inhumanities, such wholesale deportations of peoples into slavery, such annihilations of minorities.* The terror of Torquemada pales before the Nazi Inquisition. These deeds are the overshadowing historical facts by which generations to come will remember this decade. If we cannot eliminate the causes and prevent the repetition of these barbaric events, it is not an irresponsible prophecy to say that this twentieth century may yet succeed in bringing the doom of civilization.[93]

References

[1] *Documents on British Foreign Policy 1919-1939*, edited by E.L. Woodward and Rohan Butler, Third Series, vol.vii, 1939, (London, 1954), p. 257.

[2] *The New York Times*, October 18, 1942, p. 6.

[3] Lochner, Louis P., *What About Germany?* (New York: Dodd, Mead & Co., 1942), pp. 1-4.

[4] "Testimony of Mr. Louis P. Lochner, taken at Berlin, Germany, on 25 July 1945, by Colonel John H. Amen, IGD", The National Archives, Record Group no. 238, pp. 12-17. For the full text of Lochner's testimony cf. Appendix VII.

[5] *Current Biography*, (New York, 1942), p. 524.

[6] *Ibid.*, pp. 524-525.

[7] *Ibid.*, p. 526.

[8] *Ibid.*, p. 525.

[9] *Ibid.*

[10] Hoffmann, Peter, *The History of the German Resistance 1933-1945*, translated from the German by Richard Barry (Cambridge, Mass.: The MIT Press, 1977), pp. 214-215.

[11] *Ibid.* Also, Lochner, Louis P., *Always the Unexpected* (New York: Macmillan, 1956), pp. 294-295.

[12] Schaleben, Joy, *Getting the Story Out of Nazi Germany: Louis P. Lochner*, in *Journalism Monographs*, Number Eleven (June, 1969), p. 5.

[13] Cf. Lochner's obituary in *The New York Times*, January 9, 1975.

[14] Lochner, Louis P., *What About Germany?* pp. 1-5.

[15] "Testimony of Mr. Louis P. Lochner, taken at Berlin, Germany, on 25 July 1945, by Colonel John H. Amen, IGD", p. 12. In his testimony too, Lochner did not refer to the delivery of the document to the British Embassy in Berlin.

[16] *Documents on British Foreign Policy 1919-1939*, p. 257.

[17] *Ibid.*, pp. 316-317.

[18] There is still some uncertainty as to how the prosecution obtained a copy of the document. Lochner's "Testimony" indicates that the prosecution possessed not the original, but an English version, most probably that of Lochner's and offers no proof that it was submitted by Lochner. The "L" stood not for Lochner but for London where the group of documents designated "L" had been assembled (*Trial of the Major War Criminals Before the International Military Tribunal*, hereafter *IMT*, vol. ii, p. 277). The prosecution's declaration that the document came "through the medium of an American newspaperman [i.e. Louis P. Lochner]" (*IMT*, vol., II, p. 286), and Lochner's own confession to Byford-Jones that he was "responsible for the delivery" of the document (cf. W. Byford-Jones, *Berlin Twilight*, London, Hutchinson & Co., 1946, p. 177) are somewhat general and unspecific statements. Furthermore, the prosecution also stated that ". . . upon discovering this first document [i.e., L-3] the prosecution set out to find better evidence of what happened on this day" (cf. *IMT.*, vol. II, p. 286). It therefore stands to reason to assume that the prosecution already possessed a copy of the document, obtained either from the British or the U.S. archives, before it actually interrogated Lochner.

[19]Cf. Appendices I, II and III for the content of this document.

[20]For the contents of both documents cf. Appendices IV and V.

[21]*IMT*, vol. ii, pp. 285-287.

[22]*Ibid.*, pp. 291-292.

[23]Full text in *IMT*, vol xli, pp. 16-25.

[24]*IMT*, vol. xiv, pp. 43-47.

[25]*Ibid.*, vol. ii, p. 286.

[26]*Documents on German Foreign Policy 1918-1945*, Series D (1937-1945), vol. vii, (Washington, 1956), Appendix I, p. 559. This document entitled "Extracts from the Notebook of Colonel General Halder August 14-September 3, 1939" is identified as "Nuremberg document NOKW 3140; Case 12, Prosecution Exhibit 1359". The text of the document is preceded by the following note:

> The whole notebook, which covers the period 14 August 1939 to 24 September 1942, was lodged as an exhibit in the case against von Leeb *et al.* Short extracts were subsequently published in *Trials of War Criminals before the Nuremberg Military Tribunals,* U.S. Government Printing Office (Washington, 1951), vols. X and XI.
>
> The notebook, which consists of shorthand notes made personally by Halder in connection with his daily tasks as Chief of the General Staff of the Army, should not be confused with the official War Diaries kept by the High Command of the Army. The transcript of the notes, which were written in the Gabelsberger system of shorthand, was prepared by the staff of the Office of the U.S. Chief of Counsel for War Crimes (OMGUS).
>
> All those entries which deal primarily with matters of purely military interest have been omitted. All omissions are indicated by a series of dots. The translation has been revised to tally more exactly with the somewhat telegraphic style of the original. Some of the explanatory information supplied in the footnotes provided by the American editors at Nuremberg, who worked over the shorthand text with General Halder, has been used; these footnotes are marked with an asterisk. All the footnotes have been numbered in daily series. (*Ibid.*, p. 551).

[27]*Ibid.*, p. 205.

[28]*Nazi Conspiracy and Aggression* (Washington, 1946), vol. vii, p. 753.

[29]*IMT*, vol. xiv, p. 46.

[30]*Ibid.*, p. 45.

[31]*Ibid.*

[32]*Ibid.*

[33]*Ibid.*

[34]*Ibid.*, p. 64.

[35]*Ibid.*, P. 65.

[36]*Ibid.*, p. 45.

[37]*Ibid.*, vol. ii, p. 286.

[38]"Testimony of Mr. Louis P. Lochner, taken at Berlin, Germany, on 25 July 1945, by Colonel John H. Amen, IGD", pp. 7-8.

[39]Ger van Roon, *German Resistance to Hitler*, translated by Peter Ludlow, (London, 1971), p. 121.

[40]For a partial list of such informants, cf. Lochner, Louis P., "My 'Spies' in Naziland" in *Signature* (The Diners' Club of America Magazine), November, 1966, pp. 48-51, 116, 118, 120-122, 124, 127-128, 133.

[41]"Testimony of Mr. Louis P. Lochner, taken at Berlin, Germany, on 25 July 1945, by Colonel John H. Amen, IGD", p. 6.

[42]*Ibid.*, pp. 7-8.

[43]Groscurth, Helmuth, *Tagebücher eines Abwehroffiziers 1839-1940*, ed. by Helmut Krausnick and Harold C. Deutsch ("Quellen und Darstellungen zur Zeitgeschichte",19) (Stuttgart, 1970), pp. 179-180.

[44]Gisevius, Hans Bernd, *To the Bitter End*, translated from the German by Richard and Clara Winston (Cambridge, Mass.: The Riverside Press, 1947), p. 361. It seems somewhat unlikely that Canaris could have taken down Hitler's entire speech "word for word". Obviously, what Gisevius meant was that Canaris's original notes were far more extensive than the extant versions (cf. *Ibid.*, pp. 361-62).

[45]Baumgart, Winfried, "Zur Ansprache Hitlers vor den Führern der Wehrmacht am 22. August 1939", in *Vierteljahrshefte für Zeitgeschichte*, 16(1968), pp. 127-128, 139; and, Hermann Boehm/Winfried Baumgart, "Zur Ansprache Hitlers vor den Führern der Wehrmacht am 22. August 1939", *Ibid.*, 19(1971), pp. 301-304.

[46]Later, similar doubts were also expressed, notably by Telford Taylor and William L. Shirer. But neither author has questioned the overall authenticity of the document and their skepticism seems to have stemmed from that of the prosecution: "Still a fourth and more highly colored version [L-3], from journalistic sources, was also published at Nuremberg; this, too, is sufficiently like the others so that it cannot be dismissed as spurious, but its author is unknown and it bears the marks of exaggeration through hearsay and repetition" (Taylor, Telford, *Sword and Swastika*, [New York, Simon and Schuster, 1952], p. 295). Inadvertently identifying L-3 as C-3, William L. Shirer has written: "At Nuremberg there was some doubt about a fourth account of Hitler's speech, listed as N.D. C-3 [sic] (NCA [Nazi Conspiracy and Aggression], VII, pp. 752-54), and though it was referred to in the proceedings the prosecution did not submit it in evidence. While it undoubtedly rings true, it may have been embellished a little by persons who were not present at the meeting at the Berghof" (Shirer, William L., *The Rise and Fall of the Third Reich*, [New York, Simon and Schuster, 1960], footnote on p. 529).

[47]Gisevius, Hans Bernd, *op,cit.*, p. 361.

[48]*Documents on British Foreign Policy 1919-1939*, p. 257.

[49]*IMT*, vol. xiv, p. 44.

[50]Calic, Edouard, *Unmasked*, with a Foreword by Professor Golo Mann, translated from the German by Richard Barry (London: Chatto & Windus, 1971), p. 11. German edition: Calic Edouard, *Ohne Maske*, (Frankfurt, 1968).

[51]*Ibid.*, p. 13.

[52]*Ibid.*, p. 14.

[53]*Ibid.*

[54]*Ibid.*

[55]*Ibid.*, p. 15.

[56]*Ibid.*

[57]*Ibid.*

[58]*Ibid.*

[59]*Ibid.*, p. 78.

[60]*Ibid.*, p. 79.

[61]*Ibid.*, pp. 79-80.

[62]*Ibid.*, pp. 80-81 (emphasis added). The original German of the Armenian phrase reads: "oder erinnern Sie sich doch an die Ausrottung Armeniens" (cf. Calic, Edouard, *Ohne Maske*, Frankfurt, 1968, p. 101) which can also be rendered as: "and remember the eradication of Armenia."

[63]As quoted by Robert Cecil, *The Myth of the Master Race: Alfred Rosenberg and Nazi Ideology*, (London, 1972), p. 200.

[64]Rosenberg, Alfred, *Der Mythus des zwangstigsten Jahrhunderts*, (Munich, 1930), p. 213.

[65]Picker, Henry, *Hitlers Tischgespräche im Führerhaptquartier*, 3rd edn., (Stuttgart: Seewald, 1977), p. 422.

[66]*IMT*, vol. ix, p. 617. For a more elaborate account by Rosenberg on the "downfall" of the Persians, see *Alfred Rosenberg: Selected Writings*, edited and introduced by Robert Pois, (London: Jonathan Cape, 1970), pp. 44-47.

[67]Hauner, Milan, *Hitler: A Chronology of his Life and Time*, (New York: St. Martin's Press, 1983), p. 28. Despite the suppression of the news from Armenia, the Armenian massacres were known in Germany. Dr. Hohannes Lepsius, the authoritative historian of the Armenian holocaust, "spared neither time nor effort to drum up public opinion both in Germany and abroad against the inhuman policy of the Porte" and "launched a massive campaign to acquaint clerical and journalistic circles in the Reich with the brutal conduct of the Turks" (cf. Trumpener, Ulrich, *Germany and the Ottoman Empire, 1914-1918*, Princeton, Princeton University Press, 1968, pp. 218, 220 respectively). Lepsius's *Bericht über die Lage des armenischen Volkes in der Türkei*, printed as a manuscript in Potsdam, "was distributed during the summer of 1916 to thousands of people in Germany" (Trumpener, U., *Germany and the Ottoman Empire, 1914-1918*, p. 240. In Chapter VII of this same book, U. Trumpener has given an account of the activities of Lepsius and other concerned individuals and organizations; of the official line taken by the German government vis a vis Lepsius and the Armenian massacres; and, of the concerns expressed in the Reichstag during discussions on the Treaty of Brest-Litovsk, for the fate of the Armenian survivors of the massacres). From the very first day of its publication, *Der Orient* (Monatsschrift für die Wiedergeburt der Länder des Ostens, Potsdam, 1919-1939; absorbed by *Evangelische Missions-Zeitschrift*) and some other periodicals published reports and eye-witness accounts of the Armenian massacres. A collection of official dispatches, selected from the literally hundreds of reports of death and destruction in Armenia, compiled by German diplomatic personnel throughout the Ottoman empire, was published immediately after the war, a period which saw the appearance of numerous books on the subject. The following is only a partial list of such publications: Lepsius, J., *Bericht über die Lage des armenischen Volkes in der Türkei*, (Potsdam: Tempelverlag, 1916); Lepsius, J., *Der Todesgang des armenischen Volkes. Bericht über das Schicksal des armenischen Volkes in der Türkei während des Weltkrieges*, (Potsdam: Der Tempelverlag, 1919); Lepsius, J., *Deutschland und Armenien, 1914-1918. Sammlung diplomatischer Aktenstücke*, (Potsdam: Der Tempelverlag, 1919); Sommer, E., *Die Wahrheit über die Leiden des armenischen Volkes in der Türkei während des Weltkrieges*, (Frankfurt/Main, 1919); Wegner, A. *Offener Brief an den Präsidenten der Vereinigten Staaten von Nord-Amerika, Herrn Woodrow Wilson, über die Austreibung des armenischen Volkes in die Wüste*, (Berlin: Buchdruck, A. Sayffaerth, [1919]); *Der Prozess Talaat Pascha*, (Berlin: Deutsche Verlagsgesellschaft für Politik und Geschichte, 1921); Künzler, J., *Im Lande des Blutes und der Tränen. Erlebnisse in Mesopotamien während des Weltkrieges*, (Potsdam: Tempel-Verlag, 1921); Lehmann-Haupt, T., *Erlebnisse eines 12-jährigen Knabens*

während der armenischen Deportation, (Potsdam, 1921); Deutscher Hülfs-bund für christliches Lieberwerk im Orient, *Armeniens Schicksal. Seine Freunde und seine Feinde*, (Frankfurt/Main, 1927); Christoffel, E., *Von des Heilandes Brüdern und Schwestern. Bilder aus evangelischer Missionsarbeit im Orient*, (Berlin-Friedenau: Christliche Blindenmission im Orient, 1930); Christoffel, E., *Zwischen Saat und Ernte. Aus der Arbeit der Christlichen Blindenmission im Orient*, (Berlin-Friedenau: Christliche Blindenmission im Orient, 1933).

[68]Trumpener, Ulrich, *Germany and the Ottoman Empire 1914-1918*, (Princeton: Princeton University Press, 1968), p. 207, note 19.

[69]As quoted by Robert Cecil, *The Myth of the Master Race: Alfred Rosenberg and Nazi Ideology*, (London, 1972), p. 41.

[70]Trumpener, Ulrich, *op.cit.*, p. 209.

[71]*Ibid.*, p. 230. For Scheubner-Richter's consular reports consult Lepsius, Johannes, *Deutschland und Armenien 1914-1918*, (Potsdam, 1919). Hitler's words about the extermination of the Armenians are reminiscent of expressions used by Scheubner-Richter in a dispatch from Erzerum dated 28 July, 1915 describing the ultimate objective of the Young Turks: "Von den Anhängern letzterer (der schoffren Richtung des jung-türkischen Komitees) wird übrigens unumwunden zugegeben, dass das Endsiel ihres Vorgehens gegen die Armenier die ganzliche Ausrottung derselben in der Türkei ist. 'Nach dem Kriege werden wir keine Armenier mehr in der Türkei haben', ist der wörtliche Ausspruch einer massgebenden Persönlichkeit" (Lepsius, *Deutschland und Armenien 1914-1918*, p. lxxvii. For full text of the document, see *ibid.*, p. 113): "The supporters of the latter (the harsh line policy of the Young Turk Committee), by the way, make no bones about the fact that the ultimate objective of their actions against the Armenians is their total extermination in Turkey. 'After the war no Armenians will be left in Turkey', are the very words of a leading figure."

[72]Cf. Trumpener, Ulrich, *op.cit.*, particularly Chapter VI ("Dissension over Transcaucasia, 1918"), pp. 167-199 and Chapter VII ("The Armenian Persecutions"), pp. 200-270.

[73]Karpat, Kemal H., "Turkish Soviet Relations" in *Turkey's Foreign Policy in Transition 1950-1974*, by Kemal H. Karpat and Contributors, (Leiden, 1975), p. 77.

[74]Karabekir, Kâzim, *Cihan Harbine neden girdik, nasıl girdik, nasıl idare ettik*, vol. ii, (Istanbul, 1937), p. 30.

[75]Karpat, Kemal H., *Turkey's Politics*, (Princeton: Princeton University Press, 1959), p. 24.

[76]_____, "Turkish Soviet Relations", p. 78.

[77]*Ibid.*

[78]Hostler, Charles Warren, *Turkism and the Soviets*, (London, 1957), p. 177.

[79]*Ibid.*, p. 184.

[80]*Nazi Conspiracy and Aggression*, vol. iv, (Washington, 1946), p. 57 (document 1517-PS).

[81]*Ibid.*, pp. 70-71 (document 1520-PS).

[82]Howard, Harry N., "Germany, The Soviet Union, and Turkey during World War II", in *The Department of State Bulletin*, July 18, 1948, pp. 71-72.

[83]Ataöv, Türkkaya, *Turkish Foreign Policy 1939-1945*, (Ankara, 1965), p. 131.

[84]Howard, Harry N., *op.cit.*, p. 72.

[85]*Ibid.*, p. 71.

[86]Çavdar, Tevfik, *Talat Paşa*, (Ankara, 1984), p. 496.

[87]*Ibid.*, p. 343.

[88]'Trumpener, Ulrich, *op.cit.*, p. 231.

[89]Franz von Papen, *Memoirs*, trans. by Brian Connell, (New York: E.P. Dutton & Co., 1953).

[90]Hostler, Charles Warren, *op.cit.*, p. 171.

[91]*Ibid.*, pp. 172-175.

[92]Çavdar, Tevfik, *op.cit.*, p. 496. In general, there emerged at this period a trend to vindicate the discredited and blood-stained regime of the Young Turks. The Pan-Turanist fantasy, closely associated with the Young Turks, experienced a strong revival. Talaat's body was returned. The first Turkish edition of Talaat's "memoirs" appeared in 1946. Hüseyin Cahit (Yalçın), a Young Turk and a very close associate of Talaat, published a biography of Talaat in 1943. Cahit's booklet was in effect an attempt to rehabilitate the Young Turks and Talaat.

[93]*IMT*, vol. xix, p. 397 (emphasis added).

Appendices

I. The text below is the English version of the German document handed to Louis P. Lochner in Berlin. It first appeared in Lochner's *What About Germany?* (New York: Dodd, Mead & Co., 1942), pp. 1-4. The Nuremberg Tribunal later identified the document as L-3 or Exhibit USA-28. Two other versions of the same document appear in Appendices II and III. For the German original cf. *Akten zur Deutschen Auswärtigen Politik 1918-1945*, Serie D, Band VII, (Baden-Baden, 1956), pp. 171-172.

My decision to attack Poland was arrived at last spring. Originally, I feared that the political constellation would compel me to strike simultaneously at England, Russia, France, and Poland. Even this risk would have had to be taken.

Ever since the autumn of 1938, and because I realized that Japan would not join us unconditionally and that Mussolini is threatened by that nit-wit of a king and the treasonable scoundrel of a crown prince, I decided to go with Stalin.

In the last analysis, there are only three great statesmen in the world, Stalin, I, and Mussolini. Mussolini is the weakest, for he has been unable to break the power of either the crown or the church. Stalin and I are the only ones who envisage the future and nothing but the future. Accordingly, I shall in a few weeks stretch out my hand to Stalin at the common German-Russian frontier and undertake the redistribution of the world with him.

Our strength consists in our speed and in our brutality. Genghis Khan led millions of women and children to slaughter — with premeditation and a happy heart. History sees in him solely the founder of a state. It's a matter of indifference to me what a weak western European civilization will say about me.

I have issued the command — and I'll have anybody who utters but one word of criticism executed by a firing squad — that our war aim does not consist in reaching certain lines, but in the physical destruction of the enemy. Accordingly, I have placed my death-head formations[1] in readiness — for the present only in the East — with orders to them to send to death mercilessly and without compassion, men, women, and children of Polish derivation and language. Only thus shall we gain the living space (*Lebensraum*) which we need. Who, after all, speaks today of the annihilation of the Armenians?

Colonel-General von Brauchitsch has promised me to finish the war in Poland in a few weeks. Had he reported that I need two years or even only one year to do it, I should not have issued the order to march but should have allied myself temporarily with England instead of with Russia. For we are not in a position to carry on a long war.

One thing is true: a new situation has now been created.[2] I got to know those wretched worms, Daladier and Chamberlain, in Munich. They will be too cowardly to attack. They won't go beyond a blockade. We, on the other hand, have our *autarky* (self-sufficiency) and the Russian raw materials.

Poland will be depopulated and then settled by Germans. My pact with Poland[3] was, after all, intended only to gain time. And as for the rest, gentlemen, the same thing will occur as regards Russia that I have tested out (*durchexerziert*) in the case of Poland. After Stalin's death — he is a very sick man — we shall demolish the Soviet Union. The dawn of German domination of the world will then break.

The little states cannot scare me. Since Kemal's death Turkey is being governed by cretins and semi-idiots. Carol of Rumania is a thoroughly corrupt slave of his sexual desires. The King of Belgium and the Nordic kings are soft jumping jacks, dependent upon the good digestion of their gorged and tired peoples.

We shall have to count on Japan's reneging. I have given Japan a full year's time. The emperor is a counterpart of the last czar. Weak, cowardly, undecided. May he fall a victim to the revolution! My cooperation with Japan never was popular anyway.

We shall continue to stir up unrest in the Far East and in Arabia. Let our mentality be that of lords of the creation (*Herren*) and let us see in these peoples, at best, lacquered semi-apes who crave to be flogged.

The opportunity is favorable as never before. My only apprehension is that Chamberlain or some other such dirty cuss (*Saukerl*) may come at the last moment with proposals and appeasements. I'll throw such a fellow down the stairs, even if I have to kick him in the belly before all photographers.

No, it's too late for that.[4] The attack upon and the annihilation of Poland begins early on Saturday. I'll let a couple of companies, dressed in Polish uniforms, make an assault in Upper Silesia or in the Protectorate. It's a matter of utter indifference to me whether or not the world believes me. The world believes in success alone.

For you, gentlemen, glory and honor are in the offing, such as have not beckoned for centuries. Be tough! Be without compassion! Act more quickly and more brutally than the others! The citizens of western Europe must shudder in horror. That's the most humane method of conducting war, for that scares them off.

The new method of conducting war corresponds to the new draft of the frontiers — one continuous rampart from Reval, Lublin, and Kosice to the mouth of the Danube. The rest will be awarded to the Russians. Ribbentrop has instructions to make every offer and to accept every demand.

In the west I reserve to myself the fixing of the best strategic frontier. There one can operate with Protectorates, say of Holland, Belgium, French Lorraine.

And now: at the enemy! In Warsaw we shall meet again and celebrate!

[1]Meaning the special SS military formations.
[2]Apparently Hitler refers to the nonagression pact with Russia.
[3]January 26, 1934.
[4]Evidently meaning compromise.

II. The following is the English text of the German document, identified at Nuremberg as L-3 or Exhibit USA-28, which Louis P. Lochner delivered to the British Embassy in Berlin. Sir George Ogilvie-Forbes of the British Embassy forwarded the document to his government on 25 August, 1939. The text is taken from *Documents on British Foreign Policy 1919-1939*, Edited by E.L. Woodward and Rohan Butler, Third Series, vol. vii, (London, 1954), pp. 258-260. For the German original cf. *Akten zur Deutschen Auswärtigen Politik 1918-1945*, Serie D, Band VII, (Baden-Baden, 1956), pp. 171-172.

Contents of the Speech by the Führer to the Chief Commanders and Commanding Generals on the Obersalzberg, August 22, 1939.

Decision to attack Poland was arrived at in spring. Originally there was fear that because of the political constellation we would have to strike at the same time against England, France, Russia and Poland. This risk too we should have had to take. Göring had demonstrated to us that his Four-Year Plan is a failure and that we are at the end of our strength, if we do not achieve victory in a coming war.

Since the autumn of 1938 and since I have realised that Japan will not go with us unconditionally and that Mussolini is endangered by that nitwit of a King and the treacherous scoundrel of a Crown Prince, I decided to go with Stalin. After all there are only three great statesmen in the world, Stalin, I and Mussolini. Mussolini is the weakest, for he has been able to break the power neither of the crown nor of the Church. Stalin and I are the only ones who visualise the future. So in a few weeks hence I shall stretch out my hand to Stalin at the common German-Russian frontier and with him undertake to redistribute the world.

Our strength lies in our quickness and in our brutality; Genghis Khan has sent millions of women and children into death knowingly and with a light heart. History sees in him only the great founder of States. As to what the weak Western European civilisation asserts about me, that is of no account. I have given the command and I shall shoot everyone who utters one word of criticism, for the goal to be obtained in the war is not that of reaching certain lines but of physically demolishing the opponent. And so for the present only in the East I have put my death-head formations[1] in place with the command relentlessly and without compassion to send into death many women and children of Polish origin and language. Only thus we can gain the living space that we need. Who after all is today speaking about the destruction of the Armenians?

Colonel-General von Brauchitsch has promised me to bring the war against Poland to a close within a few weeks. Had he reported to me that he needs two years or even only one year, I should not have given the command to march and should have allied myself temporarily with England instead of Russia for we cannot conduct a long war. To be sure a new situation has arisen. I experienced those poor worms Daladier and Chamberlain in Munich. They will be too cowardly to attack. They won't go beyond a blockade. Against that we have our autarchy and the Russian raw materials.

Poland will be depopulated and settled with Germans. My pact with the Poles was merely conceived of as a gaining of time. As for the rest, gentlemen, the fate of Russia will be exactly the same as I am now going through with in the case of Poland. After Stalin's death — he is a very sick man — we will break the Soviet Union. Then there will begin the dawn of the German rule of the earth.

The little States cannot scare me. After Kemal's death Turkey is governed by 'cretins' and half idiots. Carol of Roumania is through and through the corrupt slave of his sexual instincts. The King of Belgium and the Nordic kings are soft jumping jacks who are dependent upon the good digestions of their over-eating and tired peoples.

We shall have to take into the bargain the defection of Japan. I gave Japan a full year's time. The Emperor is a counterpart to the last Czar — weak, cowardly, undecided. May he become a victim of the revolution. My going together with Japan never was popular. We shall continue to create disturbances in the Far East and in Arabia. Let us think as 'gentlemen' and let us see in these peoples at best lacquered half maniacs who are anxious to experience the whip.

The opportunity is as favourable as never before. I have but one worry, namely that Chamberlain or some other such pig of a fellow ('Saukerl') will come at the last moment with proposals or with ratting ('Umfall'). He will fly down the stairs, even if I shall personally have to trample on his belly in the eyes of the photographers.

No, it is too late for this. The attack upon and the destruction of Poland begins Saturday[2] early. I shall let a few companies in Polish uniform attack in Upper Silesia or in the Protectorate. Whether the world believes it is quite indifferent ('Scheissegal'). The world believes only in success.

For you, gentlemen, fame and honour are beginning as they have not since centuries. Be hard, be without mercy, act more quickly and brutally than the others. The citizens of Western Europe must tremble with horror. That is the most human way of conducting a war. For it scares the others off.

The new method of conducting war corresponds to the new drawing of the frontiers. A war extending from Reval, Lublin, Kaschau to the mouth of the Danube. The rest will be given to the Russians. Ribbentrop has orders to make every offer and to accept every demand. In the West I reserve to myself the right to determine the strategically best line. Here one will be able to work with Protectorate regions, such as Holland, Belgium and French Lorraine.

And now, on to the enemy, in Warsaw we will celebrate our reunion.

The speech was received with enthusiasm. Göring jumped on a table, thanked blood-thirstily and made bloodthirsty promises. He danced like a wild man. The few that had misgivings remained quiet. (Here a line of the memorandum is missing in order no doubt to protect the source of information.)[3]

During the meal which followed Hitler said he must act this year as he was not likely to live very long. His successor however would no longer be able to carry this out. Besides the situation would be a hopeless one in two years at the most.[4]

---

[1]The S.S. Death's Head formations were principally employed in peace-time in guarding concentration camps. With the S.S. Verfügungstruppen they formed the nucleus of the Waffen S.S.

[2]August 26.

[3]This sentence in brackets forms part of the original typescript.

[4]A fuller account of Herr Hitler's two speeches at Obersalzberg on August 22 is printed in The Trial of the Major War Criminals before the International Military Tribunal, Nuremberg, 1947, et seq., Vol. XXVI, Documents PS 798 and 1014. The summary printed above is also printed in Nazi Conspiracy and Aggression, U.S. Government Printing Office, 1946, Vol. VII, Document L3, in a slightly different translation. Another version is printed in The Trial of the Major War Criminals, Vol. XLI, Document Raeder 27.

III. Reproduced below, from *Nazi Conspiracy and Aggression*, vol. vii, (Washington, 1946), pp. 752-754, is an English rendition of the German document which came into Louis P. Lochner's hand in Berlin. At Nuremberg, this document was identified as L-3 or Exhibit USA-28. For the German original cf. *Akten zur Deutschen Auswärtigen Politik 1918-1945*, Serie D., Band VII, (Baden-Baden, 1956), pp. 171-172.

TRANSLATION OF DOCUMENT L-3
CONTENTS OF HITLER'S TALK TO THE SUPREME COMMANDER AND COMMANDING GENERALS, OBERSALZBERG, 22-8-39.

Decision to attack Poland in the spring. Originally it was feared that due to political combinations, England, Russia, France, and Poland had to be fought against simultaneously. Even this risk would have had to be borne. Goering has stated that the Four Year Plan had failed and that we were at the end if we were not victorious in the coming year.

Since Autumn, 1938, and since, I have found out that Japan does not go with us without conditions, and that Mussolini is menaced by the weak-headed king and the treacherous scoundrel of a Crown Prince. I have decided to go with Stalin. On the whole, there are only three great statesmen in the world: Stalin, myself, and Mussolini. Mussolini, the weakest, has not been able to break either the power of the crown or of the church. Stalin and I are the only ones that see only the future. So I shall shake hands with Stalin within a few weeks on the common German-Russian border and undertake with him a new distribution of the world.

Our strength is in our quickness and our brutality. Ghengis Khan had millions of women and children killed by his own will and with a gay heart. History sees only in him a great state builder. What weak Western European civilization thinks about me does not matter. I have given the order and will have every one shot, who utters even one word of criticism that the aim of the war is not to attain certain lines, but consists in the physical destruction of the opponent. Thus for the time being I have sent to the East only my "Death's Head Units" with the order to kill without pity or mercy all men, women, and children of Polish race or language. Only in such a way will we win the vital space

49

that we need. Who still talks nowadays of the extermination of the Armenians?

Colonel General [Generaloberst] von Brauchitsch has promised me to bring the war against Poland to a conclusion within a few weeks. If he would have told me that it would take me two years or even one year only, I would not have issued the order to march and would have temporarily entered into an alliance with England instead of Russia. For we cannot conduct a long war. In any case, a new situation has now been created. I have witnessed the miserable worms Daladier and Chamberlain in Munich. They will be too cowardly to attack. They will not go any further than blockade. Against it we have our autarchy and the Russian raw materials. Poland will be depopulated and colonized with Germans. My pact with Poland was only meant to stall for time. And besides, gentlemen, in Russia will happen just what I have practiced with Poland. After Stalin's death (he is seriously ill), we shall crush the Soviet Union.

The small countries do not frighten me. After Kemal's death, Turkey will be ruled by morons and half-idiots. Carol of Rumania is a thoroughly corrupted slave of his sexual desires. The King of Belgium and the Northern kings are weak puppets, depending on the good digestion of their over-fed and tired peoples.

We must take into account the defection of Japan. I have left to Japan a whole year's time to decide. The Emperor is the companion piece of the late Czars. Weak, cowardly, irresolute, he may fall before a revolution. My association with Japan was never popular. We will furthermore cause unrest in the Far East and Arabia. Let us think of ourselves as masters and consider these people at best as lacquered half-monkeys, who need to feel the knout.

The occasion is favorable now as it has never been. I have only one fear and that is that Chamberlain or such another dirty swine comes to me with propositions or a change of mind. He will be thrown downstairs. And even if I must personally kick him in the belly before the eyes of all the photographers.

No, for this it is too late. The invasion and the extermination of Poland begins on Saturday morning. I will have a few companies in Polish uniform attack in Upper Silesia or in the Protectorate. Whether the world believes it doesn't mean a damn to me. The world believes only in success.

Glory and honor are beckoning to you, gentlemen, as they

never did for centuries. Be hard. Be without mercy. Act quicker and more brutally than the others. The citizens of Western Europe must quiver in horror. That is the most human warfare for it scares them off.

The new warfare corresponds to the new border status. A wall from Reval, Lublin, Kaschau to the Danube Estuary. The Russians get the rest. Ribbentrop has received instructions to make any offer and to accept any demand. In the West, I reserve the right to ascertain the line strategically best. Here, there will be something to do with Holland, Belgium, French Lorraine as protectorate areas.

And now, on to the enemy! In Warsaw, we will celebrate our meeting again.

The speech was listened to enthusiastically. Goering jumped on the table. Bloodthirsty thanks and bloody promises. He danced around like a savage. The few doubtful ones remained silent.

During the meal, Hitler stated that he must operate this year, as he would not be living long. His successor would not be able to do so; furthermore, the situation would be desperate in two years at the latest.

IV. The following text of Nuremberg Document 798-PS or Exhibit USA-29 appears in *Documents on German Foreign Policy 1918-1945*, Series D (1937-1945), vol. vii, (Washington, 1956), pp. 200-204:

Nuremberg Document 798-PS
Exhibit USA-29
Unsigned Memorandum
SPEECH BY THE FÜHRER TO THE COMMANDERS IN CHIEF ON AUGUST 22, 1939.[1]

I have called you together to give you a picture of the political situation, in order that you may have some insight into the individual factors on which I have based my decision to act and in order to strengthen your confidence.

After this we shall discuss military details.

It was clear to me that a conflict with Poland had to come sooner or later. I had already made this decision in the spring, but I thought that I would first turn against the West in a few years, and only after that against the East. But the sequence of these things cannot be fixed. Nor should one close one's eyes to threatening situations. I wanted first of all to establish a tolerable relationship with Poland in order to fight first against the West. But this plan, which appealed to me, could not be executed, as fundamental points had changed. It became clear to me that, in the event of a conflict with the West, Poland would attack us. Poland is striving for access to the sea. The further development appeared after the occupation of the Memel Territory and it became clear to me that in certain circumstances a conflict with Poland might come at an inopportune moment. I give as reasons for this conclusion:

1. First of all two personal factors:

My own personality and that of Mussolini.

Essentially all depends on me, on my existence, because of my political talents. Furthermore, the fact that probably no one will ever again have the confidence of the whole German people as I have. There will probably never again in the future be a man with more authority than I have. My existence is therefore a factor of great value. But I can be eliminated at any time by a criminal or a lunatic.

The second personal factor is the Duce. His existence is also decisive. If anything happens to him, Italy's loyalty to the alliance will no longer be certain. The Italian Court is fundamentally opposed to the Duce. Above all, the Court regards the expansion of the empire as an encumbrance. The Duce is the man with the strongest nerves in Italy.

The third personal factor in our favour is Franco. We can ask only for benevolent neutrality from Spain. But this depends on Franco's personality. He guarantees a certain uniformity and stability in the present system in Spain. We must accept the fact that Spain does not as yet have a Fascist party with our internal unity.

The other side presents a negative picture as far as authoritative persons are concerned. There is no outstanding personality in England and France.

It is easy for us to make decisions. We have nothing to lose; we have everything to gain. Because of our restrictions [*Einschränkungen*] our economic situation is such that we can only hold out for a few more years. Göring can confirm this. We have no other choice, we must act. Our opponents will be risking a great deal and can gain only a little. Britain's stake in a war is inconceivably great. Our enemies have leaders who are below the average. No personalities. No masters, no men of action.

Besides the personal factors, the political situation is favourable for us: In the Mediterranean, rivalry between Italy, France and England; in the Far East, tension between Japan and England; in the Middle East, tension which causes alarm in the Mohammedan world.

The English Empire did not emerge stronger from the last war. Nothing was achieved from the maritime point of view. Strife between England and Ireland. The Union of South Africa has become more independent. Concessions have had to be made to India. England is in the utmost peril. Unhealthy industrialization. A British statesman can only view the future with concern.

France's position has also deteriorated, above all in the Mediterranean.

Further factors in our favour are these:
Since Albania, there has been a balance of power in the Balkans, Yugoslavia is infected with the fatal germ of decay because of her internal situation.

Rumania has not grown stronger. She is open to attack and vulnerable. She is threatened by Hungary and Bulgaria. Since

Kemal's death, Turkey has been ruled by petty minds, unsteady, weak men.

All these favourable circumstances will no longer prevail in two or three years' time. No one knows how much longer I shall live. Therefore, better a conflict now.

The creation of Greater Germany was a great achievement politically, but militarily it was doubtful, since it was achieved by bluff on the part of the political leaders. It is necessary to test the military [machine]. If at all possible, not in a general reckoning, but by the accomplishment of individual tasks.

The relationship with Poland has become unbearable. My Polish policy hitherto was contrary to the views of the people. My proposals to Poland (Danzig and the Corridor) were frustrated by England's intervention. Poland changed her tone towards us. A permanent state of tension is intolerable. The power of initiative cannot be allowed to pass to others. The present moment is more favourable than in two or three years' time. An attempt on my life or Mussolini's could change the situation to our disadvantage. One cannot for ever face one another with rifles cocked. One compromise solution suggested to us was that we should change our convictions and make kind gestures. They talked to us again in the language of Versailles. There was a danger of losing prestige. Now the probability is still great that the West will not intervene. We must take the risk with ruthless determination. The politician must take a risk just as much as the general. We are faced with the harsh alternatives of striking or of certain annihilation sooner or later.

Reference to previous hazardous undertakings.

I should have been stoned if I had not been proved right. The most dangerous step was the entry into the neutral zone. Only a week before, I got a warning through France. I have always taken a great risk in the conviction that it would succeed.

Now it is also a great risk. Iron nerves, iron resolution.

The following special reasons fortify me in my view. England and France have undertaken obligations which neither is in a position to fulfil. There is no real rearmament in England, but only propaganda. A great deal of harm was done by many Germans, who were not in agreement with me, saying and writing to English people after the solution of the Czech question: The Führer succeeded because you lost your nerve, because you capitulated too soon. This explains the present propaganda war. The English speak of a war of nerves. One factor in this war of nerves is to boost the increase of armaments. But what are the real facts about British rearmament? The naval construction programme for 1938 has not yet been completed. Only the reserve fleet has been mobilized. Purchase of trawlers. No substantial strengthening of the Navy before 1941 or 1942.

Little has been done on land. England will be able to send at most three divisions to the Continent. A little has been done for the Air Force, but it is only a beginning. Anti-aircraft defence is in its initial stages. At the moment England has only 150 anti-aircraft guns. The new anti-aircraft gun has been ordered. It will take a long time before sufficient numbers have been produced. There is a shortage of predictors. England is still vulnerable from the air. This can change in two or three years. At the moment the English Air Force has only 130,000 men, France 72,000, Poland 15,000. England does not want the conflict to break out for two or three years.

The following is typical of England. Poland wanted a loan from England for her rearmament. England, however, only granted credits in order to make sure that Poland buys in England, although England cannot make deliveries. This suggests that England does not really want to support Poland. She is not risking eight million pounds in Poland, although she poured five hundred millions into China. England's position in the world is very precarious. She will not take any risks.

France is short of men (decline in the birth rate). Little has been done for rearmament. The artillery is obsolete. France did not want to embark on this adventure. The West has only two possibilities for fighting against us:

1. Blockade: It will not be effective because of our autarky and because we have sources of supply in Eastern Europe.

2. Attack in the West from the Maginot line: I consider this impossible.

Another possibility would be the violation of Dutch, Belgian and Swiss neutrality. I have no doubt that all these States, as well as Scandinavia, will defend their neutrality with all available means. England and France will not violate the neutrality of these countries. Thus in actual fact England cannot help Poland. There still remains an attack on Italy. Military intervention is out of the question. No one is counting on a long war. If Herr von Brauchitsch had told me that I would need four years to conquer Poland I would have replied: "Then it cannot be done." It is nonsense to say that England wants to wage a long war.

We will hold our position in the West until we have conquered Poland. We must bear in mind our great production capacity. It is much greater than in 1914-1918.

The enemy had another hope, that Russia would become our enemy after the conquest of Poland. The enemy did not reckon with my great strength of purpose. Our enemies are small fry. I saw them in Munich.

I was convinced that Stalin would never accept the English offer. Russia has no interest in preserving Poland, and Stalin knows that it would mean the end of his régime, no matter whether his soldiers emerged from a war victorious or vanquished. Litvinov's replacement was decisive. I brought about the change towards Russia gradually. In connection with the commercial treaty we got into political conversations. Proposal for a non-aggression pact. Then came a comprehensive proposal from Russia. Four days ago I took a special step, which led to Russia replying yesterday that she is prepared to sign. Personal contact with Stalin is established. The day after tomorrow von Ribbentrop will conclude the treaty. Now Poland is in the position in which I wanted her.

We need not be afraid of a blockade. The East will supply us with grain, cattle, coal, lead and zinc. It is a mighty aim, which demands great efforts. I am only afraid that at the last moment some swine or other will yet submit to me a plan for mediation.

The political objective goes further. A start has been made on the destruction of England's hegemony. The way will be open for the soldiers after I have made the political preparations.

Today's announcement of the non-aggression pact with Russia came as a bombshell. The consequences cannot be foreseen. Stalin also said that this course will benefit both countries. The effect on Poland will be tremendous.

In reply, Göring thanked the Führer and assured him that the Wehrmacht would do their duty.

[1]According to the prosecution at the International Military Tribunal of Nuremberg; on May 17, 1946, this document and No. 193 came originally from the files of the OKW see *Trial of the Major War Ciminals before the International Military Tribunal* (Nuremberg, 1947-1949) (hereinafter cited as *Trial of the Major War Criminals*), vol. xiv, pp. 64-65. Another record of what Hitler said at the Obersalzberg on Aug. 22, made at the time by General Admiral Hermann Boehm, was submitted to the International Military Tribunal as Exhibit Raeder-27 and is printed in *op. cit.*, vol. xii, pp. 16-25. See also document No. 193, and Appendix I, entry for Aug. 22.

V. Reprinted below is the text of Nuremberg Document 1014-PS or Exhibit USA-30, taken from *Documents on German Foreign Policy 1918-1945*, Series D (1937-1945), vol. vii, (Washington, 1956), pp. 205-206:

Nuremberg Document 1014-PS
Exhibit USA-30

Unsigned Memorandum[1]

SECOND SPEECH BY THE FÜHRER ON AUGUST 22, 1939

Things can also work out differently regarding England and France. It is impossible to prophesy with any certainty. I am expecting an embargo on trade, not a blockade, and furthermore that relations will be broken off. The most iron determination on our part. No shrinking back from anything. Everyone must hold the view that we have been determined to fight the Western Powers right from the start. A life and death struggle. Germany has won every war when she was united. An inflexible, unflinching bearing, above all on the part of superiors, firm confidence, belief in victory, overcoming the past by becoming accustomed to the heaviest burdens. A long period of peace would not do us any good. It is therefore necessary to be prepared for anything. A manly bearing. It is not machines that fight each other, but men. We have the better men as regards quality. Spiritual factors are decisive. On the opposite side they are weaker men. The nation collapsed in 1918 because the spiritual prerequisites were insufficient. Frederick the Great only achieved final success by his fortitude.

The destruction of Poland has priority. The aim is to eliminate active forces, not to reach a definite line. Even if war breaks out in the West, the destruction of Poland remains the priority. A quick decision in view of the season.

I shall give a propagandist reason for starting the war, no matter whether it is plausible or not. The victor will not be asked afterwards whether he told the truth or not. When starting and waging a war it is not right that matters, but victory.

Close your hearts to pity. Act brutally. Eighty million people must obtain what is their right. Their existence must be made secure. The stronger man is right. The greatest harshness.

Swiftness in making decisions is necessary. Firm faith in the German soldier. Crises are due solely to leaders having lost their nerve.

First requirement: Advance up to the Vistula and the Narev. Our technical superiority will shatter the nerves of the Poles. Every newly formed active Polish force is to be destroyed again immediately. A continuous process of attrition.

New German frontier delimitation according to sound principles and possibly a protectorate as a buffer state. Military operations will not be influenced by these considerations. The wholesale destruction of Poland is the military objective. Speed is the chief thing. Pursuit until complete annihilation.

Conviction that the German Wehrmacht is equal to all demands. The order for the start of hostilities will be given later, probably Saturday morning.

---

[1]See document No. 192. A further account of this speech is contained in a document, designated L-3, which was referred to but not submitted in evidence by the prosecution at the International Military Tribunal, and therefore not published in the official record. An English translation will be found in *British Documents*, Third Series, vol. vii, No. 314, enclosure. See also *ibid.*, No. 399.

VI. Colonel General Halder's notes for 22 August, 1939, are taken from "Extracts from the Notebook of Colonel General Halder, August 14 - September 3, 1939", published as Appendix I in *Documents on German Foreign Policy 1918-1945*, Series D (1937-1945), vol. vii, (Washington, 1956), pp. 551-572. The notes for 22 August, 1939 appear *Ibid.,* pp. 557-559.

22 AUGUST 1939
Führer Conference (Obersalzberg, 1200)[1]
Present: The Army Group and Army Commanders of the three Armed Forces.

I. *Exposition of the situation, and decision* (Morning)

1) *Development of the decision* to settle Eastern question: theoretically desirable to settle with West first, but as it has become increasingly clear that Poland would fall on us from behind in any difficult situation the Eastern question must be disposed of before the problems in the West are tackled.

2) *Germany's present position* favourable for settlement of Eastern question. A number of factors are in our favour now which would not exist a few years hence.

(a) *Personal considerations:*

On our side: the personality of the Führer.—The personality of Mussolini as the sole champion of the imperial idea. Proved his strength in Abyssinian conflict. The personality of Franco, the champion of unified progressive leadership and of friendship for Germany in Spain.

On the enemy's side: there are no men of the necessary calibre to carry through, firmly and heroically, the very difficult decisions which must be taken, especially on the English side. The enemy has much to lose [whereas we] only stand to gain.

(b) *Political advantages:*

England is contained: in the *Mediterranean*, by tension with Italy: in the Far East, by tension with Japan; in Near East, by tension with the Mohammedan peoples.

England did not win in the last war. In entering a new war the Empire must reckon with changes in its structure.

France's position has also deteriorated. Decline in birth-rate.

Balance of forces in *Balkans* since Albania, Yugoslavia tied down. Rumania vulnerable and dependent on the tension between the other Powers. Turkey has no leadership.

"A showdown, which it would not be safe to put off for four

to five years, had better take place now.

"Use of military weapons necessary, before final great showdown with West: testing the [military] machine.

"A general settlement of accounts is not desirable, but rather disposing of specific issues; this is not only politically but also militarily the right way."

(c) *Poland:*

Polish-German relations unbearable. Proposals concerning Danzig and communications through Corridor (Currency question) were turned down at England's instigation. Settlement of Polish tension must not be left to solution by third powers. Time for solution now ripe, therefore strike! Political risk involved cannot be avoided. No great decision without risk.

3) *Reasons leading to [this] decision*

Only two States (England and France) can feel any obligation to assist Poland, England primarily, France towed in England's wake.

England's rearmament has not yet altered the situation substantially in England's favour. Improvement of Navy will not be noticeable until 41/42: on land it will also take considerable time for effects to be felt; only air force improved. Today England's vulnerability in the air is still great. Therefore England desires armed conflict only in three to four years' time.

France's armaments partially outdated, but not bad. Population dwindling. France cannot afford long war.

In the West there remain only two possibilities:

Blockade: Unpromising, as we can utilize Danube basin.

Attack in West:

(*a*) Attack on West Wall psychologically impossible, also militarily very difficult.

(*b*) Violation of neutral States. These countries really wish to remain neutral. Besides, England also needs their neutrality.

Therefore we expect that England and France will not violate neutrality. Military intervention therefore without prospects. "Long war" not attractive. Germany can be expected to do better in a long war now than in 1914.

Russia will never be so senseless as to fight for France and England.

Developments: Dismissal of Litvinov:[2] sign of ending of policy of intervention; commercial treaty.[3] Even before that, conversations, on Russia's initiative, on non-aggression pact,[4] intervention in Russo-Japanese conflict, Baltic States.

Russians have informed [us] that they are prepared to conclude pact. Personal contact Stalin-Führer. "With this I have knocked the weapons out of the hands of these gentry [*Herrschaften*]. Poland has been manoeuvred into the position that we need for military success."

Ultimate effect cannot yet be foreseen: new course! Stalin writes[5] that he expects a great deal for both sides. Tremendous revolution in the whole European political situation.

II. The Führer's demands on his military chiefs

1) *Ruthless determination:* Anglo-French counter moves will come. We must stand fast. Build-up in West will go forward [*W-Aufmarsch wird gefahren*]. "Iron steadfastness of all in authority."

2) *Aim: Annihilation of Poland* — elimination of its vital forces. It is not a matter of gaining a specific line or a new frontier, but rather of the annihilation of an enemy, which must be constantly attempted by new ways.

3) *Solution:* Means immaterial. The victor is never called upon to vindicate his actions. We are not concerned with having justice on our side, but solely with victory.

4) *Execution:* Harsh and remorseless. Be steeled against all signs of compassion!

Speed: Faith in the German soldier even if reverses occur!

Of paramount importance are the wedges [which must be driven] from the south-east to the Vistula, and from the north to the Narev and Vistula. Promptness in meeting new situations; new means must be devised to deal with them quickly.

5) *New frontiers:* New Reich territory? Outlying protectorate territory. Military operations must not be affected by regard for future frontiers.

III. Details

1) Probable start: Saturday morning.

2) Slovakia (List):[6] Instruct Barckhausen to strengthen Slovak frontier defence. Elements of 7th Air Force Division to Zipser-Neudorf. Slovak airmen to be grounded. We guarantee Slovakia against Hungarians taking action.[7]

3) Dirschau: Attack at dawn on Y-day by dive-bomber groups

on western end of bridge and town (barracks, power plant, etc.). Simultaneously freight train [*Bahnzug*] from Marienburg, followed by armoured train and remainder of [group] Medem.

4) Gdynia: Air attack simultaneously with Dirschau; simultaneous blockade of harbour.

5) Operation of Army *Reichenau*:[8] No comment.

6) Review of position of enemy in sector of Army Group North.

[1] See also documents Nos. 192 and 193.

[2] See vol. vi of this Series, document No. 325.

[3] See document No. 131.

[4] See document No. 50.

[5] See document No. 159.

[6] Colonel General Siegmund Wilhelm List, C-in-C Fourteenth Army, in Army Group South (Slovakia).

[7] See document No. 214.

[8] *Tenth Army, in Army Group South (Upper Silesia).

VII. Lochner's interrogation took place while he was recuperating from an accident in Berlin:

As I was driving along one of Berlin's broadest boulevards in mid-June of 1945, a Russian truck, coming down the boulevard on my left, made a sudden, unannounced left turn and crashed into my jeep. I was in the hospital for four weeks with a concussion of the brain, a lacerated cheek, a wound in the calf of my right leg, and a badly cut eyelid. (Lochner, Louis P., *Always the Unexpected*, New York, Macmillan, 1956, p. 283).

Lochner then stated that he "was released on the very day on which the Potsdam agreement was made public —August 2nd" (*Ibid.*, p. 284). There is some discrepancy here: Lochner's hospitalization must have been longer than four weeks, or the accident must have occurred later than mid-June. Nevertheless, the definite date of Lochner's release and his concluding statement in his testimony below allow us to assume safely that he was interviewed at the American military hospital.

The original of Lochner's Testimony is at The National Archives, Record Group No. 238.

Testimony of Mr. Louis P. Lochner, taken at Berlin, Germany, on 25 July 1945, by Colonel John H. Amen, IGD.

THE WITNESS WAS SWORN

Q   Will you please state your full name?

A   Louis P. Lochner.

Q   What is your present occupation?

A   I am war correspondent for the Associated Press.

Q   For how long a time have you been so employed?

A   As war correspondent, only since October of last year.

Q   You were the chief of the Associated Press office in Berlin for a period of time?

A   I was an editor from 1924 to 1928 and chief of bureau from 1928 to 1942.

Q   And you spent a considerable portion of your life in Germany?

A   21 years. Three years preceding 1924, when I had been here as a free-lance, and I had previously frequently visited Europe.

Q   Your wife was German?

A   My wife is German born, and has been an American citizen since 1922.

Q   And you have children?

A   I have three children.

Q   Have they spent a substantial portion of their lives in Germany?

A   All three received their primary education in Berlin, and two of them then went to the University of Chicago for finishing their education, whereas the third one, the daughter, became a clerk in the American Embassy after finishing what would correspond to a high school, in Germany.

Q   In the course of the performance of your duties, did you frequently come in contact with German Government officials?

A   It was naturally my duty to cultivate just as many Government officials as possible, in order to have as full a view as possible of the news developments in this country, no matter what the regime was or might be.

Q   Were you personally acquainted with many of those officials?

A   You mean the Nazi officials, in the present case?

Q   Yes.

A   I knew practically the whole top hierarchy of the Nazi Government. Due to the fact that I was not only here as Associated Press correspondent, but for six years had been President of the Foreign Press Association, which naturally involved many official contacts, and had been president of the American Chamber of Commerce in Germany.

Q   Did those officials include Schacht?

A   Yes.

Q   Von Papen?

A   Yes.

Q   Hugenberg?

A   Yes.

Q   And what others, particularly?

A   Hitler, Goering, Himmler, Goebbels, Ley, Funk — successor to Schacht — Rust, the educational minister; Kerrl, minister of Church affairs; Seldte, minister of labor; Von Blomberg, minister of war; Von Schwerin-Krosigk, finance minister; and that is about the lot.

Q   Did you know all of these individuals personally?

A   Yes, I knew them all personally, and I dare say most of them knew me personally, although naturally I think some of them I had only few dealings with, so that I would be introduced to them, and they may have forgotten me, but certainly they knew my name.

Q   In the course of the performance of your duties, did there ever come to your attention, a German manuscript entitled: "Contents of Speech to the Supreme Commanders and Commanding Generals, Obersalzberg, August 22, 1939?"

A   Yes, sir, that was brought to me.

Q   Approximately when and under what circumstances was that first brought to your attention?

A   Naturally I had from the very beginning of the Nazi regime, I had built up a system of information and contacts and communications aside from the regime, because we realized that what was being spoon-fed to us by the propaganda ministry and foreign office, as the two chief dispensers of information to the foreign press, was anything but the truth. And so, through my long acquaintance also with leading men of the Weimar Republic I was in a position to build up this system, and I believe that those who staunchly still stood for the Republic, were aware where my sympathies were, and I never made any bones about it, and the Government also knew that I was anything but enraptured with the Nazi regime; so, sometimes in a rather surprising manner, even men whom I hardly knew personally nevertheless sent information to me. One of these cases was Colonel General Beck.

Q   Do you recall his first name?

A   I think it is Joseph. In my book, by the way, I think I give the name. Colonel General Beck, the former Chief of Staff of the German Army who, however, resigned because of differences with Hitler at least a year before the World War began. Beck seemed tremendously concerned about what Hitler was leading Germany into and, therefore, had information sent to me from time to time by a gentleman who was known to me from the Democratic Youth Movement of Republican days — a certain Herr Maasz, but I don't remember his first name — in whose integrity I certainly believed and still believe if he is alive, and so he sent me this manuscript through this Mr. Maasz.

Q   What was Mr. Maasz's position or duties?

A   Mr. Maasz was a merchant. He was selling paper, I believe. That is, after he had been removed by the Nazis from his position in the youth work that was going on during the Weimar Republic, such as running a number of youth hostelries where youth traveling from town to town could be, and things of that sort, but he had always been in some form or other in what you might call the German underground. He was staunchly anti-Nazi and was doing everything he could to let the outside world know what Hitler was leading the Germans into.

Q   What was his connection, if any, with Colonel General Beck?

A   It seemed simply that he belonged to a series of underground contacts that people of like mind, I mean who were all anti-Nazi, had with each other, and as he was a civilian, perhaps it seemed least surprising that he could come into me in my office. We always had arranged on what we have talked about in case somebody questioned afterwards. Sometimes it was selling papers, and sometimes he had some plans for printing letter-heads for me, but he was always there on business.

Q   Had he previously acted as an intermediary between you and Colonel General Beck?

A   Yes, he had acted previously and always gave me little bits of information indicating in what direction Hitler was running. For instance, at the time of the rearmament of the Rhineland, I knew that in advance that Hitler was going to take that step, and Beck thought the French would surely march at that time and prevent it. Yes, he had given me valuable information from time to time, which always proved reliable.

Q   And in these other instances how had you learned that he was acting on behalf of Colonel General Beck?

A   I took him on his faith. He told me that, and through still other circles I knew that I had been recommended to General Beck as an anti-Nazi who could be trusted.

Q   Had you ever discussed Mr. Maasz with Colonel General Beck?

A   No. I had only met Colonel General Beck at a dinner once, and we sat next to each other and we had exchanged things, but that was before he had begun to come to me with these things. It may be because — I don't know whether in that evening he got a fine impression of me, but that is the one and only time I remember being together with Colonel General Beck.

Q   Had Maasz always been the person who brought you this information from Colonel General Beck?

A   Yes.

Q   No one else?

A   No one else. No.

Q   Now, coming back to this particular manuscript of August 22 1939, when and under what circumstances was that first brought to your attention?

A   Mr. Maasz came to me as he had often done before, into my office.

Q   Where was your office located?

A   That was down in Zimmer Strasse, SSE 68, in the newspaper row, where the various big concerns are. Opposite us was the German News Bureau and so on. He came to me and this day particularly was sure that the room was closed, and I had an inside office and nobody could see us, and then he produced this thing.

Q   Was there anyone else in the room at the time?

A   No, there was nobody with me. He produced it to me and first read it out to me and then when he came to a few words that I just don't know what they were, he took his scissors and cut those out and said, "Well, here is one name mentioned in here, and if ever this manuscript fell into the wrong hands, they would know where this comes from." It was evidently the person who took the stenogram of that meeting, and he cut that out, and after having read it out to me, he handed it to me, and I have been in possession of it ever since. It was possibly three, and possibly lapped over on the fourth page, but I think it was three pages — in which he said this man, a higher officer, not one of the highest and, therefore, sitting in the rear ranks of the officers present at the Hitler meeting, had begun to take down in shorthand on his white cuffs of his uniform, or of the shirt, and at first only in abbreviated sentences; and then when he realized what the import of it was, then he began to expand those sentences, and so in the original you will find — give me the wording there —

(Colonel Amen hands document to witness)

— You will find it saying, for instance, "My decision to attack Poland arrived last Spring. Originally feared political constellation would compel me to strike simultaneously at England, Russia, France, and Poland." Naturally, in putting this out in book form, I filled in the sentences to read: "My decision to attack Poland was arrived at last spring." Put in the predicate. "Originally I feared that the political constellation would compel me to strike simultaneously at England, Russia, France, and Poland." In other words, I in no way changed the sense of it, only I filled out the sentences. But about the beginning of the

4th paragraph: "Our strength consists in our speed and in our brutality." etc., he began to write the thing out in full, and from there on there are no abbreviated sentences in my original manuscript that I have.

Q   You say that this was approximately a three-page manuscript?

A   Yes.

Q   And it was written in German?

A   Written in German.

Q   Part of it was in shorthand notes?

A   No, not shorthand notes, but it was abbreviated sentences, as I said before that. I understand the officer took down shorthand, and writing very small, first on a cuff, and then I don't know what he did later with it, but the transcript that I received was first in the form of broken off sentences and then as it goes on and the story becomes hotter, then in full sentences.

Q   Did Maasz give you the name of the officer who had been present at the meeting and taken this down?

A   No. That is the name that I am under the impression he cut out when he read it over a second time, and did not want to get the man into trouble.

Q   The manuscript which you have has the space cut out where a name was previously located?

A   Yes, sir.

Q   The quotation to which you were referring, in the answer to my last questions, was a quoted speech on pages 4, 5 and 6 of the document which I handed you?

A   Yes, sir.

Q   Did you change the sense, or otherwise edit the document, except to insert words which would complete sentences?

A   I did nothing otherwise to change it; no.

Q   Was the translation which is reflected in the quoted document which I show you, your own personal translation?

A   That is my personal translation, and after 21 years in Germany I flatter myself into really knowing German, and if necessary even being able to write a book in German.

Q   Where is the original manuscript today?

A   It must be in my apartment at 45 Prospect Place, Tudor City, New York.

Q   Can you suggest how we could get hold of that original manuscript in the quickest possible way?

A   Assuming that I have it in there, it should be in my wardrobe trunk, to which Mrs. Lochner, who is living there and awaiting my return, has the keys. As I remember it, I left it in a cellophane cover together with several other documents in which the Department of Justice some months ago had an interest, and in which these documents were returned by the Department, together with the request, if possible, to leave them in there so that I might handily grasp them in case I was summoned to Washington for testimony. I only hope that I haven't in the last confusion of my suddenly leaving for Europe, done something different with them, but I seem to remember I put them into the wardrobe trunk and left them in the cellophane.

Q   Would it be feasible for you to send word to Mrs. Lochner to see if she can locate them and deliver them to some authorized representative of ours?

A   That would be possible, surely.

Q   Do you plan to return to the States yourself in the near future?

A   I am hoping so. My plans are upset by my accident here, and my agreement with the home office was that I really was to keep Berlin as my last assignment and then to go home and resume broadcasting work, but at this moment I have no means of knowing just what that means.

Q   To the best of your knowledge and recollection, does the quotation which I have shown you conform exactly to the translation which you made of the original? (Handing document to witness.)

A   It appears to be an exact copy of the wording of my translation as I published it in my book, "What About Germany."

Q   When Mr. Maasz brought you this manuscript in your office, what conversation did you have with him, other than what you have already stated?

A   He was greatly shocked at the brutality of the whole statement and told me that Colonel General Beck had also been, when he received it. He thought at the time that it would be a mighty fine thing if the American State Department were advised of it, and if they possibly could in some way or other use it in a publicity way to show up the Hitler regime. He knew that I could not publish it from Berlin and still remain at my post. I then talked to the American Embassy but unfortunately the charge d'affaires in charge at that time declined to have anything to do with it.

69

Q   Do you recall what his name was?

A   It was Alexander Kirk, who is now Ambassador in Italy; and he said to me, "Oh, take this out of here. That is dynamite." And I said, "Yes, but the American Government ought to know about this whole thing." And he said, "Oh, we have had so many troubles already, I don't want to get involved. I don't know whether our code isn't known, etc." And he simply declined to accept it.

Q   What were the circumstances under which the manuscript was shown to the Department of Justice representatives?

A   The Department of Justice had a case in Washington of a number of people under indictment for subversive activities. As I remember it, there were a number of out-spoken Nazis among them, but I forget the particular case, and it seems that the Department had also seen this chapter in my book with this statement, and desired to fit that into the picture of the whole trial, so that is why they sent an agent from Washington to ask me how I had come to write this chapter, and what the background was, and I think I gave very much according to what I am telling you now, except at that time I doubt whether I involved even Colonel General Beck personally, as he was still alive then, and I had no knowledge of what the publicity might do to him then. I have no hesitation now, as he has been executed.

Q   Do you recall the name of the agent who came to talk to you about this?

A   No, I am sorry, I don't.

Q   But your recollection is that he came from Washington?

A   Yes.

Q   To Hollywood?

A   To Hollywood.

Q   Do you recall approximately when that was?

A   I think it was in the spring of 1944, but it may have been earlier. There you really have me. My life has gone so fast with me that I am mixed up on my dates. I would hate to go on record positively on that.

Q   Was he an agent of the Federal Bureau of Investigation, do you recall?

A   He came with an F.B.I. man from Los Angeles, whose name I also don't remember, but I don't think he was called a special agent of the F.B.I., but a special agent of the Department of Justice. I remember and I recall that there was a difference in the two titles.

Q There were two individuals who came?

A Yes.

Q One from the F.B.I. in Los Angeles, and the other from Washington?

A Yes.

Q Did they take any formal statement from you?

A No, they took — they were interested in the material and I showed them some other documents that I thought were interesting, as casting a light upon the mendacity of the Nazi regime, and it was this material that they afterwards — again using the local F.B.I. agent — asked me to entrust to them to send to Washington, so that they might obviate the necessity of my coming down. Then, when it was returned they said, "Leave it together in case we need it."

Q Did you deliver this original manuscript to them at the time when they called on you?

A I did.

Q Then how did you get it back again?

A It came in this cellophane enclosure together with other documents.

Q Through the mails?

A No, sir, it was delivered by an agent again.

Q To your home?

A To my home; yes.

Q Were you ever called upon to testify, either before a Grand Jury, or otherwise?

A No.

Q Do you recall what trial it was that they were then interested in? Was it a trial on the coast, or in Washington?

A A trial in Washington, D.C.

Q Of a group of saboteurs?

A I don't think it was the saboteurs so much as subversive activity that these people were charged with.

Q Do you recall who any of the persons charged, were?

A Well, there was that dame who — what did she do? She jumped up and kissed somebody, or heiled Hitler, or some fool thing.

Q Oh yes, I recall.

A It is easy to identify by that incident. As I said before, there were some Nazi-lovers trying to make a nuisance of themselves

71

throughout the trial.

Q Do you recall whether it was the trial, in the course of which Judge Eicher died, and a mistrial was declared?

A I never followed the end of the thing. I never even knew that the judge had died.

Q Do you know whether the manuscript was introduced in evidence at the trial?

A No, I don't know.

Q In any event, you were not called to testify at the trial?

A No.

Q You will note that on page 4 of the document which I have shown you, it states that a photostat of this speech is marked Exhibit 2. Do you know to what photostatic copy reference is there being made? Did you give these agents any photostatic copy, or did they make any photostatic copy?

A They must have made some, because they returned these to me. They labeled this Exhibit 2, and sent the original back to me, and I think when these were returned, they did have numbers of exhibits on it. If it was "2" or not, I don't know, but I think that was the only alteration they took on my stuff, was that mark then, in that sequence.

Q You never did learn the name of the individual officer who made the notes?

A No. As far as I can remember, I don't think I did. It was one of those things that I did not press them, knowing the danger and risks involved, and I had infinite confidence in both the man who had sent Maasz, and Maasz himself, as he had always proven reliable previously, and I knew Maasz through a period of years.

Q When Mr. Maasz brought this document to your office, did he say anything about Colonel General Beck, other than what you have already mentioned?

A No, I don't think so, because the main purpose was the document itself. That spoke for itself. Only the General's great concern about what Hitler was doing.

Q Did he say that Colonel General Beck had given him the manuscript, or merely had suggested that he give the manuscript to you?

A As I recall it, Maasz merely said, "I am coming once again from Colonel General Beck, and I have something that will certainly interest you." And then he pulled this out and began to read it to me, until he came to the name, and then he cut it out, and then afterwards handed it over to me.

Q   In the course of your conversation with Mr. Maasz, what if anything was said about Goering?

A   Well, he said — but I believe he based it on a sort of postscript to this verbatim account, that after this whole thing was read, some of the older Generals sort of in an amazed manner looked at each other, and into that silence Goering jumped on a table, and with almost delirious eyes, as I have known him to make when he gets into certain stages of ecstasy, that he had cheered this whole thing and brought out a heil sig for the Feuhrer, or something of that sort. Anyway, he led the demonstration then of the younger and what I would call the pro-war party there.

Q   Was there any conversation with Mr. Maasz, or did you otherwise learn anything about the names of the individuals who were present at this meeting?

A   No. He simply said it was for the Generalitite — before the General's Corps. That is a term that everybody understands in Germany. It means the top-ranking crowd that are summoned together for a thing of that sort.

Q   Do you recall anything other than that to which you have already testified, either about this document and its receipt by you, or any conversations which you may have had with either Mr. Maasz or Colonel General Beck about it?

A   The only thing I recall is that at a later period I did tell Maasz that unfortunately I was unable to get this sent in code to the United States at the time, but that I was keeping it in hiding, and at the first possible moment I would have, I would still use every means at my command to acquaint the American people with it. That opportunity did not come till after my release from internment — and the publishing of my book.

Q   Did you ever have occasion to exhibit the manuscript to anyone other than the Department of Justice agents, and Alexander Kirk?

A   No. I did have occasion to let somebody have a typewritten copy of it. That was when the New York agent of a liberal magazine appearing in the German language, in Chile — the name of which I have forgotten — on reading my book said that he thought it ought to be known just what German words Hitler used, and whether I was ready to furnish a copy for publication. I was very glad to do that because in every way possible I was trying to provoke some reaction from the German Government on this thing, or to put it conversely, I had already gained the impression from the English publication of it, and a rather sensational news dispatch that the Associated Press made concerning my book, in which this very thing is featured as the chief item of the news report, that the German authorities are very well acquainted with the book, and that if they had any real denial to make they would undoubtedly deny it, as it would almost have knocked the props from under my book, showing that this fellow is a liar, but nothing of the sort ever came, and so I thought once more, I will try it by the means of publishing it even in German and giving them a chance to deny it, but even that has never happened. Since coming to Germany I have now learned that the book had indeed made the rounds of a great many people in the Government circles there, and yet that nobody has ever, even in their private talks, challenged the authenticity of that document. It is very interesting to me. They took up the ethics of whether I, as a guest of the country, as they called it, might afterwards write a book of that kind, and my conduct, and so on, and some of them found it more objective than they had expected of me, in view of my stand against them, because I am trying really to present facts, and not just innuendo and propaganda, but the interesting thing is that every person who I have struck so far, and some of them were in Government offices, is that no one has challenged that document.

Q   Did there also come to your attention, in the course of the discharge of your duties, various so-called instructions from Goebbels?

A   Yes, and I am now ready even to reveal the name of the man who furnished them to me, because he too has been purged. His name was Dr. Alfred Mehlhemmer. Mehlhemmer was a man who had long been active in the Catholic Center Party, and was the lay contact man between some of the pronouncedly anti-Nazi Catholic bishops, both among themselves and among their laity. He was also a contact man over to the Protestant Confessional Center, as well as to the few Jewish rabbis who were still left in Berlin. One of these rabbis had told Mehlhemmer that I was a reliable person, and so we took up the contact. He was not himself present at these daily press conferences, as he was not a journalist, but a fellow — a coreligionist of his, was.

Q   Do you know his name?

A   No, I don't know his name, and in those days one didn't ask. It was better not be be loaded down with more names than you could carry. Through this man he received these secret press instructions. They were regarded so valuable when I, naturally as a patriotic American, turned that over to both the War Department and the State Department officials in Berlin, that the later charge d'affaires who succeeded Mr. Kirk — Mr. Morris — Mr. Leland B. Morris — told me that he had a wire from the State Department to the effect that these were the most enlightening and worthwhile things that were coming out of Germany at all, and begging me to make every effort to get as complete a dossier as I could. That was not quite possible because the informant who took down these notes was not always sent to the daily conference. Sometimes somebody else from that same office was sent, but just as complete as we could get them, we put them together and as I say, I naturally furnished a copy to the authorities.

Q   Was it your understanding that those instructions had been taken down word for word, or in shorthand, by the friend of Dr. Mehlhemmer?

A   Yes, it was my understanding; and there again from the somewhat ragged way in which sometimes sentences were completed and others were not, it looked to me like simply another likelihood of their authenticity. I know how it is when you take a thing down and new sentences start in and you could not quite catch up with it, and I was given the thing exactly as he had taken it down each day. But much more interesting proof was perhaps on the basis of his secret instruction of this kind, I would the next day ask an embarrassing question at the press conference — the amazed and surprised looks that there were, indicated to me that I hit the bull's eye. I was naturally never fool enough ever to publish them at that time because that would have meant putting the Gestapo on the definite hunt of who might be the man, and that would dry up my source. To me it was far more important that the American Government should know what the real facts are, as compared with the propaganda, and that I should know where they were heading for, so that I wouldn't fall for their propaganda, than to come out officiously — "Well, here is a transcript." I had had another sad lesson, and that was in the early days of the Nazi regime when the representative of the Manchester Guardian and also of one French paper and I, were given a transcript by the nephew of a

German general, whose name I have forgotten and the Manchester Guardian representative unfortunately, one day when he was in dearth of news, thought he would spring a sensation and published verbatim the instructions of that particular day. That led to a man hunt in the course of which this young journalist was ferreted out. They watched everybody — what everybody was doing, and where he went — and finally caught him in the act of handing it to the Frenchman, and except for the illustrious name of the general, his uncle, he would have been executed, but it was then commuted to life sentence. I learned my lesson then and never made any use of these transcripts until I came back to the United States and we were starting in the war, and then it was a very valuable asset.

Q   In what form did these instructions come into your hands?

A   They were written on the trypewriter.

Q   In German?

A   In German, and I again made the translations of these.

Q   Where are the original instructions which you received, today?

A   I think they are in that same wardrobe trunk. I think I have left my most important papers there.

Q   Were they also submitted by you to the Department of Justice agents?

A   As I remember it, only certain pertinent ones that they were interested in from the viewpoint of their trial, but my memory is not quite clear on that.

Q   Are those pertinent ones, the ones which are set forth on pages 8 and 9 of the document which I hand to you.

(Document handed to witness by Colonel Amen.)

A   Yes, those are the ones.

Q   Would it be possible for you to ask your wife to make a search for those, as well as the manuscript which we first discussed?

A   Yes, that would be quite possible.

Q   Presuming they are in the same place.

A   I imagine they are.

Q   Do I understand that the reason why you did not disclose the name of Mr. Maasz and Colonel General Beck previously was because you feared that your life might thereby be in danger?

A   It was more the lives of those men I was afraid of. No. I was out of the country, and that was all right. It wasn't my life, but their lives, and the lives of their relatives. Which is one of the terrible things the Nazis have introduced. The collective responsibility of the whole tribe or clan.

Q   Did that apply equally in the case of the instructions?

A   Yes.

Q   Have you any way of knowing whether Mr. Maasz is still alive?

A   No. I don't know, and I sometimes fear for the worst, because it has been rather remarkable how many of my old contacts have somehow or other turned up. They have somehow just gotten word around I am back in the country, and all day long there has been a procession here for the last couple of days as they will tell you outside of people turning up, and Maasz is not among them.

Q   Do you know of any leads which might be pursued in order to ascertain his whereabouts, or that of any of his relatives or friends?

A   No, I don't know, because I don't live in Berlin proper. I can't for the life of me recall the suburb — it was distinctly a suburb and not an outside burough, but a suburb of Berlin from where he came in. I asked somebody even the other day whom I thought might know him, and he did not know what had happened to him, and did not know where to trace him. But I will gladly, if I get any lead toward him, I will let you know that.

Q   Are you acquainted with Mr. Himmelsheim?

A   Yes.

Q   Would he possibly have information about Maasz, or did he know him?

A   I don't think he was in that same group. That was a different circle, and I was contacting as many different ones as I could. I want to explain in that connection, just to give you a picture of what terrible thing these people were all up against, that one did not even dare acquaint people from one circle with the next one. Not because you feared there might be a stool pigeon or anything like that, but as one of them once put it to me, "we are really carrying our small group on our consciences. We don't know what we might do either, under torture." Or, even a thing they feared even more, and that was the administering of certain poisons that break the will. That I saw used in the case of the Reichstag fire case, when Van der Lubbe was transformed in the course of a few weeks at the trial, from a rather belligerent, to an absolutely will-broken person, and they said, "We will take your word for it that this group of which you speak over here, are okay, but we would rather not know names at this moment." It is hard for outsiders, I think, to understand that situation here in Germany, but I think those who begin to get into it see it was right in not forcing names of one group on another. I think more than the torture was a fear, whether real or not — I don't know how those poisons act — but the injection of poisons to break the will.

Q   Will you glance through this document which I hand you, captioned: "Louis P. Lochner, 6726 Milner Road, Hollywood, California," or such parts thereof as you have not already read, and tell me whether you subscribe to everything which is attributed to you in this document, or if there is anything to which you do not subscribe, let me know what it is.

(Document is handed to witness by Colonel Amen.)

A   Regarding General Kaupisch, about a month ago he was living near Weimar. I saw him about a month ago and he is now much more free to talk because he was long removed. He told me an interesting thing. I made a story of it for the Associated Press. He said, the first time he ever saw the leaflets bearing his name was when they came flying down. He said, first it was an atrocious Danish, and second, it was things he would never have said. And there he said that Denmark was simply overrun. He is an honest fellow. There is one little conflict in my testimony here. I say here: "In November 1940, I was visited by a German writer whose religious convictions impelled him to relieve his conscience to the extent of imparting the Goebbels instructions to some foreigner whom he could trust." That was Dr. Mehlhemmer, but I say: "This man stated to me: 'I want you to receive the press instructions whenever I can secure them for you. I am not always sent to the conference, so there will be gaps.'" That is a mistake. "My colleague is not always sent to the conference." I am sorry I made this mistake, but it is just a lapse of memory. Now I know about his death it came to me more clearly than at the time I wrote this. The address of General Kaupisch is Bad Berka, Thuringia. You reach it by going to Weimar, and you go five miles south of Weimar to Bad Berka, and he is — it is such a small place, they would know where the general lives.

Q   It is a private house?

A   No, a boarding house, but he and his wife are living there. I would look into this because I think he could give you some in-

78

teresting information.

Q   On the Danish angle?

A   Yes, on the Danish angle. He has been discharged a long time ago. He was very skeptical throughout. They put him in charge as Governor of Denmark because in the first days they wanted to show what nice, cultured fellows they were, but he wasn't tough enough for them, so they kicked him out again. I simply have in here, "See General Kaupisch." I am quite sure in that little place, if nowhere else the police headquarters must know where he is. It is a small spot.

Q   Do you know of any other sources of information which might be helpful in the prosecution of the major war criminals?

A   I mean, just what have you in mind? I mean, witnesses? I want to help you in every way possible.

Q   Anything and everything. In other words, if you tell me any sources that occur to you, I can quickly tell you whether or not they are being covered. It just occurred to me you might know someone else like this general, whom we wouldn't be apt to run across, and whom you happen to know would have some personal knowledge.

A   Yes. I suppose you have this name of the Catholic priest who was present at all the hangings, Buchholz.

Q   I assume so, but let us have it anyway.

A   Father Peter Buchholz. He is — well, where he lives now, I don't know. He was in charge of the Ploetzensee Prison. In one night he describes 186 hangings took place, and they were supposed to hang 300, but couldn't complete the job by dawn.

Q   Do you know what the nationality of those people was, who were hanged?

A   That was July 20th. They butchered all the Germans.

Q   Can you give me the names of persons having proof in support of the proposition that it was an intentional war of aggression on the part of Germany?

A   I see. Yes.

Q   Or persons having particular knowledge of the methods used in taking over any of the smaller countries?

A   Of course, one man who knows a lot and whom we have down in Augsburg is Paul Schmidt, present chief of the Foreign Office. I suppose he has been interrogated a great deal as he knows all about that. It would be good if one could get one of these people who, sort of in fear of their families, went with the thing, and know a lot, but themselves aren't in it. It must be somebody of some character and quality you want to talk to.

Q   I will tell you what I want to do. I will leave you my name and address, and something may occur to you, or you may run across some individual. If you will just put it down on a piece of paper, then I will have it and I may immediately send someone out to talk to him.

A   Are you going to be in the Berlin area?

Q   I am all over, but my headquarters are in Paris at the moment.

A   We get a daily courier out of here to Paris, a mail plane.

Q   What about Schacht? Do you know anybody who might have information about him that would be helpful?

A   Well, the other day I was visited — but it is up to you whether it is worth anything — I was visited by the representative of Hardy and Company, the banking firm, who gave me a rather interesting story about how all the other various chief directors of the Reichsbank, Reichs Credit and Gesellschaft of the Deutsches Bank, and Berlin Handelsgesellschaft were all arrested, but he himself is not. He is a Dr. Freundt, speaks English very well, and he lives in Argentina Allee, near here, #11. At any rate, it is a house where a lot of enlisted men are now billeted, but the family has been allowed to remain upstairs. I should think that he must have had a lot of dealings with Schacht. There is one living man who lived through the war here, and therefore had dealings with him all through. I don't see why a man who makes the whole economic basis possible of a war, that he should escape the firing squad.

Q   It is not planned that they should. How about Von Papen?

A   As to who knows about him. Of course in the former days, this fellow Hummelsheim knew quite a lot about Von Papen.

Q   Of course he does.

A   But he doesn't know that last era.

Q   Yes, he has been quite helpful.

A   He is a man I would endorse. He is okay. It might be possibly that the food administrator for Berlin, Dr. Andreas Hermes, was in the same party with him at least. Of course, Papen was always the outsider in the party and he might know quite a lot about him. He is on the Russian side. They moved him forcibly out of the American zone to the Russian zone, but Hermes was long a politician in the Centerist Party and he ought to know quite a little about Von Papen's ambitions and things. A man who might know, simply from the viewpoint again of the Catholic opposition is the Professor of Journalism, Dr. Emil Dovifat, who lives right near here. He left his card, and I haven't been able to see him yet, but he is a man of great integrity, in Charlottenburg Strasse #2. Dovifat was the head of the Catholic Action Movement here and that was the lay movement, of course, and I could very well imagine if they were worth anything else, they would have also supplies in Papen's outfit, and Dovifat is a man who is absolutely honest. I know him. Then there is here also another man who again is certainly a great opponent of his, and that is Professor Herman Muckermann. He can be reached through the Kaiser Wilhelm Gesellschaft. We have taken over some of their buildings. It is a big scientific institution. I have heard to my surprise, Muckermann was in this country and alive, and now I understand why Chancellor Bruning asked me in the second edition of my book, he said that he was in some danger; and that is the only name I mentioned, because I thought he was out, you see. He also belonged to the anti-Papen Catholic crowd, but I should think between them they ought to know something about it, as they were all in politics. They are right here in town and may be contacted.

Q   May I assume, if it is so desired, you would be willing to testify and identify these documents at the trial of the major war criminals?

A   If it were desirable, yes.

Q   Have you anything further to state, or any other information to give concerning any of the matters I have questioned you about?

A   I would certainly like to be helpful, but when you have come to a patient who isn't quite up to par anyway, and who has had a concussion of the brain, I may not respond as readily as you would like to have me. I am not as clear as I ought to be, but I will be mulling this over, because naturally I am tremendously interested in this.

(END)